BECOMING DEBT-FREE

A JOURNEY TOWARDS FINANCIAL FREEDOM

RIAN GRACE

A THOUSAND WORDS A DAY

Cover Design: Gayda Estanislao

Ebook ISBN: 978-1-923262-00-3

Paperback ISBN: 978-1-923262-01-0

Hardback ISBN: 978-1-923262-07-2

❀ Created with Vellum

DISCLAIMER

The information in this book should not be used as professional financial or legal advice. The author cannot possibly account for all varying circumstances of each individual reader. Hence, what worked for the author may or may not work for the reader, depending on various confounding factors.

The author does not guarantee any results of financial decisions you make. Prior to taking any action regarding finances, it's best to conduct your own research and due diligence, or seek advice from a competent professional.

Readers are also advised that certain information in this book only applies at the time of writing, and current events may render them obsolete after publication. The author makes no representations as to the accuracy, completeness, currentness, suitability, or validity of any information in this book. The author is not liable for any errors, omissions, or delays in this information, or any losses, injuries, or damages arising from the use of this book. All information in this book is provided by the author on an "as is" basis.

CONTENTS

ACKNOWLEDGMENTS

Leo – jester, #1 fan, motivator, driver

Archie – alpha reader

Mama and Papa – beta readers

Wendy – copy-editor

Bea – proofreader

Ate Gayda – book cover designer

My friends – moral support

INTRODUCTION

Debt-free is the new black. In the world of capitalism, being debt-free is not an easy feat. While it feels good to have nice things and experience cool activities, it certainly is not worth it at the expense of anxiety due to mounds of consumer debts, on top of bigger debts like mortgages and car loans.

In this book, I share my personal finance journey from getting into too much debt to getting out of debt, and the specific things I did to keep myself consistently debt-free from the time I was able to wipe out my consumer debt at the age of 27 (more than a decade ago). I'm hoping that by writing what I've been through, people with similar attributes to mine would be able to relate and hopefully learn that if someone like me can get out of debt, so can they. This book is a testament to what a good money mindset can do to help you be free.

It is outside the scope of this book to talk about how to be rich and wealthy, whatever those words mean to you. However, we cannot deny the fact that being debt-free is a great precursor – though not mandatory – to wealth.

Time and time again, we have heard from the great gurus of the financial world that one of the tried and tested ways to accumulate wealth is by making your money work for you. Without debt and with enough disposable income to cover your living costs, you will have a greater portion of your salary allotted for investments and making money work for you. So, for now, why don't we try and be free from debt first? Or, if being completely debt-free is not an option yet, how about working our way towards freeing more of our money from debt to increase our disposable income.

What would an increased disposable income achieve? Well, you can enjoy spending it without guilt and without that constant nagging feeling at the back of your head saying, *"That amount could have gone to settling my debt instead!"*

This book is laden with stories from my time as an expatriate in the capital of the United Arab Emirates (UAE), Abu Dhabi. Interspersed among the stories are personal finance tips I've aggregated from strategies that worked for me. And although the currency I use here is mainly that of UAE dirhams (AED) with a United States dollar conversion (USD) for universality's sake, the application and lessons I share are currency blind, meaning it doesn't matter what money you're holding right now, the principles towards becoming debt-free remain the same.

WHO IS THIS BOOK FOR?

When I became an expatriate, a lot of people told me that it's possible to earn way more money for the same work that I did back home. But nobody told me about the dangers of adapting my current lifestyle according to my new income. Nobody warned me against overspending. Nobody taught me how to manage a sudden balloon in income. Nobody waved a banner saying, *"Beware, lifestyle inflation ahead!"* There's no life manual on how to control one's self from spending all their hard-earned money.

Without a heads up, it's quite easy to allow lifestyle creep without even realising it! Lifestyle creep could happen after experiencing an increase in income, wherein the spending slowly (or drastically) adjusts to match the new income figure. This is also the reason why most people who experience a promotion or move to a new higher-paying job (including expatriates who found greener pastures in another country) still end up with no savings or still remain in a lot of debt despite the increase in financial resources. The so-called luxuries in their previous lifestyle suddenly become necessities in their current lifestyle, hence, what should have been earmarked for savings or for paying down debt gets spent aimlessly again.

But just because we didn't have access to that amount of money before, doesn't mean we have to spend it all once we do. You would be surprised by the number of people who have coasted by from the year they started working up until their 50s only to wake up one day and realise that they are nearing retirement and they do not have enough for a decent nest egg, and they suddenly want to make up for all the lost years when they didn't save up. Or the number of expats who have planned to live and work in a certain country for a set period of time but have stayed two or three times longer than planned, all because they still haven't saved enough to go back home (or move to another country).

I completely understand the situation and the struggle. In one way or another, my thoughts have been constantly plagued by the worry of not being able to save enough money and being in an endless loop of employment that may or may not be to my liking. Being an expat in a country where no permanent residency or naturalisation for citizenship is given to foreign citizens (despite the years of residency) really put my personal finances into perspective. In my mind, I know that I will not and cannot stay in the UAE forever. And even though I was blessed with a terrific job at a government institution with an excellent salary package, I knew from the beginning that I must save enough for my own future because the UAE will not do it for me – there is no future pension fund awaiting my retirement in the UAE. There is no 401K (USA), Superannuation (Australia), or SSS (Philippines) equivalent, and rightly so. There is no social security waiting for me after I reach retirement age in the UAE should I choose to keep working until they kick me out when I turn 60 (some can continue working until 65 years of age with a special permit).

These are the facts that compelled me to get a good handle on my money, to avoid being knee-deep in debt, and to ensure I do not leave the UAE with an outstanding debt – because of its possible negative repercussions on my future international movements (more on this later).

If you are new to the workforce or a new expatriate and you want to avoid living a horror story about money pitfalls you have probably heard from friends or relatives; or if you have been working for far too long and have nothing substantial saved for your future, then you have come to the right place.

This book is for everyone who, in one way or another, has experienced an increase in salary and for some weird reason, doesn't know where that increase in salary went. This book is for the victims of lifestyle creep who are ready to take reins of their finances, especially those who are plagued with relentless debts; those who want to sleep peacefully at night knowing they have a firm handle on their finances; those who are ready to get rid of their excessive consumer debts so they can allocate enough money for investment and retirement; and the expats who long to come back home or move to another country where they can stay indefinitely.

I've tried my very best to be as transparent as possible with my stories, but I hope it doesn't come across as boasting. I needed to be as candid as possible so I can drive home the message that what I have achieved is possible for anyone who's willing to start, put in the effort, and stay the course.

If you are ready and 100% willing to do the work, I'm happy to be of remote assistance to your debt-free journey!

WHO IS THIS BOOK *NOT* FOR?

Some people are still enjoying the life of excessive consumerism. I sometimes like to think it is just a phase, because I was once at that stage in my life as well. When you see someone, a friend or a relative, splurging on every possible thing they can get their hands on at the expense of their credit history, let them. They are still basking in the happiness of capitalism despite mounds of debt under their belt (unless of course they are loaded, in which case, all the more that this book is not for them). No matter what you tell them, despite your concern, it doesn't guarantee they will listen. Besides, if they didn't ask you anything about how to manage their personal finances, you had better not give them any unsolicited advice. It would just come off as meddling.

If you are one of those people still savouring capitalism at this moment and you're not yet ready to let go of excessive consumption; if you're not yet prepared to detach your identity from the amount of material possessions you have; if you're not yet willing to reinvent your money habits; if you're fine living with a lot of debt and it does not really affect you mentally, then this book might not help you at the moment. You might see the concepts here as an attack against your current spending habits or money decisions even though that is not the purpose of this book.

If somebody has gifted this book to you and you're not ready to make the changes it describes, do not berate the person who gifted it to you. Instead, close the book. Keep it for now. And when you are ready to manage your finances and feel the peace of mind brought about by not having to worry about debts, come back to this book. I will still be here. The debt-free community will still be at your disposal when you are ready to be free.

SECTION ONE
GETTING INTO DEBT

There are a million ways to get into debt. At the top of my list is the age-old classic way of borrowing money: loans. You may need a loan to buy a house (mortgage) or a car (car financing). These loans allow you to borrow with a higher limit of credit and a lower interest rate compared to other types of loan because the thing you buy serves as a collateral for the money lender, be it a bank, a credit union, or any financial institution that would lend you money. These types of loan are called secured loans because of the *security* the collateral gives to the lender.

Then, there are those *untethered* loans such as personal loans, which incur a higher interest rate and a lower credit limit as compared to mortgage and car loans because they have no collateral. Depending on the country, one could also have a student loan, which is also another way of making you feel cash-strapped for an indefinite amount of time. Credit card debt – a common example of revolving debt – is also another way of getting into debt. In fact, it is one of the most common kinds of debt, after mortgage and student loans. And let's not forget about borrowing money from friends and relatives.

Taking out loans and borrowing money do *not* outright put you in a debt-ridden life, with feelings of anxiety and financial insecurity. As a matter of fact, if what you borrow is put to good use – an appreciating asset or an investment that provides dividends – then, it might even give you a stronger sense of financial security. Yes, you are technically "in debt" when you have a loan and when you borrow money, but it is not the act of borrowing that puts your personal finances in disarray, it is what you do after the borrowing that determines whether you will go broke or not.

Are you paying your debt on time? Are you still borrowing more even though you know it will make your finances even tighter? Have you resigned yourself to the fact that mounds of debts are normal and everyone else is in debt too, hence, it is completely fine for you to be in perpetual debt too?

In this first part of the book, let us dig deeper into the common ways of being in debt; how most of us underestimate the power that debt holds over us; the array of emotions associated with a ballooning debt; and all the ways a crippling debt could set us back in life.

Figure 1, below, describes the reflective approach that guided my journey to becoming debt-free. You will notice that the three bullet points in the "Being 'debtful'" phase are all in bold. This is because they form the focus of each of the following three chapters as we learn more about the process of how people get into debt.

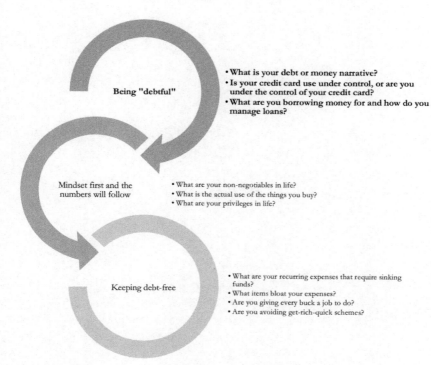

Figure 1. An overview of the reflective approach that guided my debt-free journey with the focus on being "debtful"

CHAPTER 1
HOW IT ALL STARTED

Are you tired of being in a perpetual cycle of debt? Do you have existing debts that you just can't get rid of? I want you to know you are not alone in your plight. I know a lot of other people who have been in a similar situation, which has affected their perception of debt and personal finance. Perhaps you are familiar with one or two of the following scenarios:

"I feel anxious whenever I open my banking app and I see that my balance is low on my checking and saving accounts. Add to that the high outstanding balances on my credit cards and my anxiety goes through the roof."

"Ugh. It's Monday again! I don't want to go to work! If only I didn't have bills and debts to pay, I could just quit right now!"

"I hate my job. I have a terrible boss and my colleagues are not making the working environment any better. It also looks like I'm not getting promoted any time soon, if at all. But I have to suck it up and stay in this dead-end job because I

have an EMI [equated monthly instalment] for my personal loan/mortgage/car loan, and I still have loads of credit card debt to pay off. Plus, I don't see any other employer that would pay the same salary I'm getting right now."

"I was about to fly off to another country for a leisure trip, but I got stopped at the airport because I didn't pass immigration control. Apparently, I'm on a travel ban list because of my mountains of unpaid debt."

"I want to transition to another career that I'm more passionate about. But I have to study for it, and I don't have enough savings to quit my current job and put myself through school. I wish I had enough emergency funding for situations like this."

"I want to open up a business about something that I'm passionate about. But I don't have enough savings to quit my current job and have enough capital for the business. I wish I had enough emergency funding for situations like this."

"I don't have any savings or funds for my retirement. I keep on using up all my salary to pay for my credit card debts and personal loan. Nothing gets left for savings and the future. But I'm cool with that, because as long as I keep on working, I'll have money coming in and I'll be able to afford my lifestyle. However, if I lose my job, it's going to be a struggle until I find a new one."

"I can't help myself in buying the latest things on the market, from shoes to bags to mobile phones. I've got to have all the latest gadgets and fashion trends as soon as they are released. I sometimes worry about my maxed-out credit cards, but I can't give up my lifestyle because my friends would think I'm poor if I don't have all this bling."

"I have enough disposable income to afford a little luxury here and there. I'm not in any kind of debt. However, whenever I do buy luxury items and pay for luxurious experiences, I feel uncomfortable because at the back of my mind, I keep thinking I could have added it to my retirement fund/property deposit/business capital."

"I don't need to do anything with my debt at all. I've accepted that having a lot of debt is normal. Everyone has it."

"It's normal for me to have debt because I have a family. If I were single, I could manage my income better. You, on the other hand, can easily save money because you don't have kids."

I have heard all these first-hand from people around me, sometimes a combination of two or three from the same person. It has been an ongoing narrative of people around me for as long as I can remember, which is why I thought crippling debt really was an inescapable state of life, and that financial freedom was fiction. That was the case until I started educating myself more about personal finance and how to get out of the debt trap.

If you keep seeing yourself in one of the situations above, then perhaps you can learn a thing or two from this book. If you think that being in one of the above situations is inescapable, I assure you that it's not. With the right mindset and consistent action, you won't ever find yourself stuck in any of these situations.

BUT WHY WOULD YOU TAKE MY WORD FOR IT?

First and foremost, I can completely relate to you. I have been in some of the scenarios written above. Even though I was trained as an allied health professional and worked mostly in academia, I'm no different to any other working individual in this world. Just like anyone working part time or full time, I receive money in exchange for my services. I manage that money. I spend that money. I make good, and sometimes, bad judgement calls on where to put that money. This is personal finance – the budgeting, the saving, the paying off your debts, the investing, and more. I have done all these, and more. I'm sharing the strategies in this book based on what worked for me and dozens of other people from whom I learned these money principles. Moreover, I can relate to the employed or self-employed. I'm not a one-percenter and despite my practical optimism in life, I will never be, nor do I aim to be one.

Second, I'm not going to shame you for being in debt. I'm not even going to tell you that credit is bad. Actually, I learned at a very young age that credit is the bread and butter of the economy, and individuals like you and I can also use "good" debt as a tool towards achieving financial freedom. But if you are in debt and are uncomfortable about it, mainly because of the uncertainty of your financial future, there are ways to remedy that. Nobody wants to be buried in debt now and have nothing to show for it later in life.

I remember a friend who told me that after moving from their home country to Dubai where she and her husband had significantly higher incomes, they both started maxing out their credit cards. When they decided to pay it all off – which amounted close to AED 60,000 (~USD 16,300) – and avoid the same mishap again, they looked back to that point in their lives and realised nothing had come out of it that could explain why and where they had spent such a huge amount of money. One thing is for sure though, they bought and consumed a lot of stuff which they had never done previously. This is a typical example of lifestyle creep.

In my friend and her husband's case, their consumer debts weren't so much about buying luxury items here and there. They kept buying *a lot* of low-priced items thinking everything was affordable, forgetting that even small figures add up over time. Before they realised it, they had already raked up a five-digit consumer debt during a time when they were still paying off a six-digit personal loan.

My friend was kind of disappointed that despite spending and being in debt by that much, she didn't even own a Louis Vuitton bag to show for all her money troubles! This was said jokingly of course. For her, it would have been a little bit understandable – not acceptable – to have accumulated a huge amount of debt if they had spent their money on luxury items like bags and shoes. But that wasn't the case.

It was a desperate attempt to humour themselves or to find a rationale to the question of where all their money went. And that's when it hit her. They will never let the same thing happen to them ever again because nothing, as in nothing really came out of that. But for me, as an outsider looking in, I would say that the most important thing to come out of that situation was the lesson they'd learned and the corresponding change in mindset. I'm happy to report that almost a decade after their huge debt conundrum, both my friend and her husband are still enjoying a consumer-debt-free life.

My journey towards being debt-free didn't involve starving myself and skimping on food for days on end, nor did it involve any dinners of salt and rice. I never deprived myself of my *non-negotiables in life* (more about this in another chapter), nor did I feel any discomfort during the time I was saving half of my salary. In fact, during the course of this personal finance journey of becoming and keeping myself debt-free, I was able to visit 30 countries, set up my dream business in the Philippines, gift my family and friends things I would never have thought I would be able to give in this lifetime, and more. The key was to simply focus my spending on the things and experiences I truly love, not on things and experiences that would "look good on me".

Hence, you can expect that in this book, I will not tell you to starve yourself. I will not advise you to give up your daily Starbucks. I will not discourage you from buying those limited-edition sneakers you have been coveting since their release. If these are things that really make you happy, by all means, do purchase them. As long as you don't sacrifice your peace of mind and freedom in doing so, and as long as your finances do not affect your mental health, then you're in the clear to spend your money however you want to.

If you're still not convinced and are still doubting if I really do have expertise or authority on personal finance matters, given that I have no degree that is remotely related to finance, I can sure assure you that you are right to have doubts. I'm a nobody who is financially independent. But how many nobodies do you personally know who are financially independent and who are work-optional?

I really am not an authority figure on this matter, but as a self-proclaimed personal finance geek, I hope I can provide you with some practical answers. How do you suppose I was able to find time to write this book about being debt-free? It's because I was on a self-funded sabbatical. How could I have afforded to take a self-funded sabbatical? It's because I'm debt-free. Simply put, when you're debt-free, the options are endless!

WHAT PROMPTED ME TO PURSUE BEING DEBT-FREE?

I will answer that with another question.

Have you ever experienced a morning when your alarm clock went off and you wished you didn't have to get up out of bed, and go to work? I'm quite sure we have all been in that situation at least once in our working life. That five-second-long moment upon waking up was what turned my personal finance life around from being full of debt with no savings, to debt-free with no savings, and finally to being debt-free with savings and investments.

Were you hoping that a significant or dramatic moment of epiphany caused all this? You probably thought it was going to be something exciting and excruciating at the same time, like losing all my life savings to a Nigerian prince who needed my help. Or perhaps I took a huge loan and invested everything in an obvious Ponzi scheme and lost all my money?

None of those prompted my debt-free journey. It was a simple and a very vanilla scenario of having a hard time waking up in the morning to go to work. And my income as an expat did all the legwork in eradicating my debt. (This is not to imply that only by being an expat can one eradicate debt, but this was my reality at that time.)

Mind you, I'm not a lazy person. I just wanted to have more freedom is all. When I was paying for nearly maxed out credit cards every month for approximately five years that left me without savings the entire time, I thought it was going to be a never-ending cycle. It made the mornings, all the alarms, and getting out of bed to go to work that much heavier. Waking up with a migraine compounded the heavy feeling even more.

While I loved what I was doing back then, I realised I didn't want to go to work because I needed to pay for what I'd spent the previous month. To this day, I want that when I go to work, it's not because I'm compelled by my debts or bills. I want to go to work – or not go to work – because I want to, not because I have to.

WHY DID I WRITE THIS BOOK?

As I was writing this book, I was on a self-funded year-long sabbatical in the UAE, using my golden visa to stay legally within the country, even without a job or a prospect for the next one. It was a planned sabbatical, but most of my personal projects were unplanned. Before my sabbatical started, I had a few things in mind, such as:

- study new skills;
- assist friends and relatives with executing their migration plans;
- coach interested people on personal finance management;
- travel.

During my sabbatical, I got to do all of the above. I finished *a lot* of online courses, from cybersecurity to data analytics to project management. I also helped out a few friends and relatives with their immigration applications to Australia, and I travelled extensively. But among the projects I listed above, I was most excited about the third one.

I was looking forward to doing a lot of coaching about budgeting, crushing debts, boosting savings, and the like. I cannot explain it, but somehow, helping other people manage their finances kindles an extra surge of excitement within me. If we were to use the famous Japanese concept of Ikigai (a reason for being), I guess this is deemed as passion: something I love and something I'm good at. (I'm guessing I'm good at it, otherwise, I wouldn't have any material for this book, right?) Both the work associated with managing personal finances and the outcome of having a healthy financial approach to life ceaselessly excite me. So, I offered my "financial coaching services" to most of my colleagues and friends for free. It was my way of volunteering my time, just like we all do when we want to participate in community service. Sadly, nobody signed up!

I understand. Who would actually want to confide in me and reveal sensitive information about themselves and their money habits? Personal finance is indeed a testy subject, and not everyone would be willing to expose their financial skeletons in their closet, even if it would save them.

Fortunately, a month before my sabbatical started, a colleague of mine – we will call him John – volunteered to be financially coached. His main concerns were that he had lots of debt, he had no savings, and he had not even started with his retirement fund yet even though he was already nearing 60 years old. So, I created a spreadsheet for him that tallied all his monthly recurring expenses against his monthly income. Each column corresponded to a month, with the topmost row showing his income. I dedicated a row to his one massive personal loan and placed its monthly instalment under each month's cell. I dedicated six rows to his six existing credit cards and left the cells blank as I wasn't sure if he was comfortable sharing all those figures with me. In hindsight, I should have checked with him if we could integrate those figures into the spreadsheet itself, so he was aware of the full extent of how deep his debt was because as soon as I wrote the function that showed him how much was left each month after taking out his total payables from his income, each month showed a negative figure. The figures didn't even include his six credit cards' outstanding balances, but it was quite obvious that he was already in debt. As each month went by, he was left with nothing from his salary. He even increased his debt to the bank through continued use of his six credit cards.

I strongly advised John to close all his credit cards but one. I carefully integrated all the end dates of his debt instalments so I could increase his savings rates from that month onwards. I asked him when he planned to retire and move back to his home country so I could consider his timeline in calculating his projected savings. He said he wanted to work for five more years at the time of our conversation. I made sure to put a summary of his projected savings for five years on the first worksheet with frozen columns, making it visible as soon as he opened the file or flipped onto that worksheet. I firmly believe that when you see your goals regularly, you get reminded of them and get inspired to keep focused until you achieve them.

When I sent him the tailored budget, debt, and savings spreadsheet, he jumped for joy seeing the projected savings. For the next five years, he has the capacity to save 300% of his target retirement fund! I told him that the projected savings can only be realised if he followed the two-fold plan exactly to the letter: (1) pay off all his debts and (2) start redirecting those payments towards savings (this is an oversimplification of the plan but is representative of its entirety).

Just to clarify, this person earned a decent amount of money with his full-time employment and nothing else. It really was possible to save a lot of money from his kind of salary in a short period of time, but decades of mismanaged income had led him to an inescapable cycle of debt. Even though I did the project gleefully and never judged him for all his past money decisions, I definitely sensed his defensiveness and excuses, which made his money mindset all the more obvious. For days after handing the spreadsheet to him, all he could say was how much he was looking forward to his retirement with that kind of money. He said it was such a big help to finally see his goal as opposed to just blindly saving up.

I knew for sure that John would not be able to save any money right away because his first debt instalment's end date was not until the sixth month. So, to avoid putting any pressure on him, I decided to just check in with his progress at the end of the seventh month, wherein it specifically stated on his spreadsheet that he should be able to keep AED 1,000 (~USD 270). I deliberately started with a small savings rate – so it was achievable – but programmed to increase as soon as the second debt instalment was finished. However, even with that small savings amount to start with, John wasn't able to fulfil that and started listing excuse after excuse as to why he wasn't able to save that meagre – compared to his total salary – amount for that particular month.

I immediately lost hope with his case. Here was a man in front of me, with a higher-than-average tax-free income, who was very excited about his retirement fund, but wasn't willing to take the first step towards achieving that goal. He saw a number – his projected savings – and thought he already had that amount in the bag. He didn't even exhibit the slightest change in lifestyle and money mindset to achieve his financial goal. I decided to withdraw my prompting because I knew that if John could not and did not want to help himself, I sure could not do it for him.

What happened with John's case made me reflect deeply about my passion. It made me doubt whether I'm really good at this personal finance stuff. But my own personal finance portfolio is a testament to the efficacy of what I have done to become debt-free and keep myself debt-free for the past decade and counting. I wondered whether there was a flaw in my method of delivery. Perhaps, the psychology of money has to be involved in all of it, so we cure the faulty money mindset instead of focusing on the lack of money. Mindset first, and the numbers will follow.

I realised it doesn't matter how I share the strategies that have worked for me to completely eliminate debt. It doesn't matter what medium, or how they are delivered, as long as they get shared. The further the reach, the better. So, one fine day, I opened up a word processor on my laptop and started pouring out my money practices into typewritten words. And voila! You are now holding the final product of those typewritten words. I'm hoping that this book, whether partially or in its entirety, can help you out with your personal finances. But first, let me tell you about how I got into deep debt. Perhaps, you can learn a thing or two and hopefully dodge a bullet in the process.

CHAPTER 2

MY LOVE-HATE RELATIONSHIP WITH CREDIT CARDS

How many credit cards do you currently have? One? Three? Perhaps one for each expense component that you have in your life: one card that allows rebates for petrol purchases; another card with cashback incentive for grocery purchases; another one that collects or doubles/triples/quadruples miles for air travel. Are any of these cards currently maxed out?

The maximum number of credit cards I have owned at any given point in my life is two, and that was only during the time when I thought credit cards were lifelines for emergency situations when you had an urgent need for cash or required a big purchase. It seemed as though it was an acceptable and "smart" thing to do. I was not alone in this practice. A lot of people felt secure with having a credit card "just in case". I, too, felt the same. Let's go back to my college days when I first owned a credit card, and it made me feel "safe".

MY VERY FIRST CREDIT CARD

When my parents sent me to Manila to study a five-year course in one of the big four universities, I had just enough allowance for my day-to-day expenses. Nothing more, nothing less, I think! I lived with my sister and brother in a two-bedroom apartment rental that my parents paid for. I took two jeepney rides from my apartment to my campus and took the same route back home at the end of the day. I usually ate my lunch on campus and dinner at home. So those were basically all the daily expenses I incurred: transport and food. My cash allowance, which was sent once at the end of every month, covered those two major expenses. For everything else – books, project materials, uniforms, anything related to my studies – I had to ask my mother to send extra money.

Of course, when I asked for the extra money, it didn't necessarily mean she would send the total amount in a heartbeat. I had to rationalise each and every peso required to purchase these things for my course.

My mother would say, *"What? Three books for PHP 400, 1,200, and 1,500 [~USD 7, 20, and 30]? Why don't you just buy one? Aren't they all the same?"*

At that point, I had to explain that anatomy is different from physiology and a book specifically about anatomy would not cover physiology in the depth and in a manner that we needed to know for my future profession. Or that anatomy and physiology were different from sociology. When she yielded, she would only give me money for two books instead of three. Time to photocopy the sociology one, which again, required money.

Other than books, she was also meticulous about everything I and my siblings did that cost money. *"Why do you need two more pairs of uniform when you already have three pairs? Why don't you just wash what you wore on Monday and Tuesday, so you have something to wear on Thursday and Friday?"*

You can't argue with that. But when the utility bills came: *"Why are your electricity and water bills so high? Do you always use the washing machine? How frequently do you use the washing machine? You are wasting energy and water. Just wash on the weekends!"*

I swear, it was like defending a thesis with a catch-22 situation all over.

Apart from the monthly replenished allowance kept in my bank account, the only other thing constant in my wallet was my credit card (a JCB – Japan Credit Bureau) that my parents told me to keep and use during emergency situations only. It was a supplementary card with my name on it and an PHP 85,000 credit limit (~AED 5,500 or USD 1,530). This might be nothing today, but PHP 85,000 for a 15-year-old university student back in 2002 was considered a lot of "money". Similar to treating my whole class of 40 students to lunch every day for a whole month.

My parents specifically instructed me to use it only when I really needed to buy something and when the situation was so urgent that I would not be able to wait for them to send the amount to my bank. Guess how many times I used that card in my entire five years in university? Once.

Yes, once only, and it was during my second year in university. It was for a small purchase of PHP 499 (~AED 32 or USD 9). I didn't even want to use the card at that time, but it was for an item required for my physical education (PE) course: a pair of black high-heeled leather shoes. Yes, you read that right. High-heeled shoes, preferably four inches and above.

What PE was I taking back then? Social dancing. My alma mater offered limited slots for interesting PE courses (e.g., swimming, fencing) which were easily filled up by students whose enrolment schedule were days ahead of ours. So, for the students left with no other options, we were corralled into taking the less than interesting folk dancing, social dancing, and the like.

After that purchase I never felt any "extraordinary power" in spending money I did not actually *have*. If anything, that purchase made me feel uncomfortable, despite it being a very small purchase. It was clear in my head that it was borrowed money, and my parents still had to pay for it by the end of the month. It wasn't magic. Thankfully, even though my allowance was just enough (sometimes tight even), I never felt like I was deprived in any way during my college days. So, I tucked that card away and I never used it again until after graduation (more about this later).

Sure, there were more pressing situations within those five years when I could have used the card again (e.g., typhoons that closed banks and delayed money transfers that left me with just PHP 20), but lucky for me, I had a friend who also hailed from the province who understood my situation. Whenever that friend lent me money, I made sure to pay it back as soon as my allowance came. Another handicap of my credit card was that it was a JCB. Unlike Visa or MasterCard, not a lot of establishments in the Philippines accepted JCB back then.

A YOUNG PROFESSIONAL'S DEBT SPIRAL

Fast forward to after graduation and securing three jobs in succession within less than two years of my young professional life, my salary made me eligible to certain perks from my bank, including a pre-approved credit card. During this time, I still had the supplementary credit card that my parents gave me when I was in university. Only this time, instead of an PHP 85,000 (~USD 1,530) credit limit, it was now up to PHP 150,000 (~USD 2,710). The credit increase was not based on my new status of being employed, it was based on my mother's credit history. Remember, I was a supplementary on that card.

At this point, I had a total of two credit cards: a JCB (the same credit card I had in university) and a Visa (from my salaried bank account). But I mostly used the Visa card because the JCB's monthly bill still went to my mother and no 21-year-old person would want their mother to see all their credit card purchases as they were starting to discover the world of being a young professional! Not that I did anything illegal or shameful back then, I was simply afraid my parents would find out about the lifestyle inflation I had adopted for myself. *University Rian's* mindset about how uncomfortable a credit card purchase was, had all of a sudden vanished and was replaced by the sense of security of a *salaried Rian* who received income bi-weekly.

I easily raked in a five-digit credit card debt. What for? I ate out a lot with friends and colleagues. I enjoyed trying out different cuisines and dined out almost every single night. At that time, it made sense to me. I was single and I viewed cooking for one as an ultimate waste of time when I could easily dine out and chat with friends.

Of course, shopping (e.g., for clothes, bags, accessories, etc.) was a big culprit as well. I remember buying ten pairs of shoes all in one day just because I could. Whenever I saw a style I liked, I bought them in all the colours available. All the things I bought were not even that expensive. I'm my mother's daughter anyway so I've always been a huge fan of a bargain, but you know what they say: *"Every little thing adds up."*

Then there was the "gift-giving inflation". Gone were the days when I would simply give a gift to my parents and friends on birthdays and Christmases for the sake of having something to give. I upped my game because in my head, I could afford better gifts because I was earning money from my job.

But it wasn't all consumer debt. During that time, I also enrolled myself on a master's degree, and since I didn't keep track of my expenses to see if I could really afford another degree with my salary at that time, I charged my tuition fees to my Visa card.

Doing volunteer work also entailed expenses. As a service-oriented person, I became an active member of our not-for-profit professional association that led to roles that required me to be present here, there and everywhere. Of course, getting here, there and everywhere cost money. Since we were not paid for our services to the association, all the late-night meetings at restaurants and cafes talking about how to further uplift our profession meant buying dinner and desserts out of our own pockets. Talk about labour of love.

Moreover, our duty towards the association required that our services be fairly provided nationwide wherever a provincial chapter needed our assistance in organising and promoting events geared towards professional development or creating opportunities. While the association would cover the basic expenses such as flights, board and food, it went without saying that personal expenses during those times were unavoidable. Hence, anyone volunteering for the association needed to accept that not only did it require time, but it also incurred expenses – a fact that was often overlooked from our income's point of view.

By the time I left the Philippines in 2013, I had incurred a six-digit credit card debt that just kept on growing. The two biggest mistakes that led to the ballooning of this debt were: (1) I didn't pay the full amount each month, and (2) my credit limit was higher than my monthly salary. There was no way I could ever catch up, especially with the constant eating out and shopping.

Every month, I knew I would never be able to make it, full-payment-wise. Nevertheless, I continued spending above my means and was satisfied to be able to pay the minimum amount due each month, oblivious to the fact that that is one of the fastest ways to bury oneself under a mound of crippling consumer debt.

Antidote to a possible debt spiral upon receiving your first credit card

If your bank offers you a credit card or you have applied for one, upon receiving it, make sure to watch out for these two things before starting to use it: (1) the amount of your credit limit, and (2) the annual fee.

Credit limit

Probably one of the reasons why people succumb to a lot of credit card debt is because they treat their credit limit as money they actually have. The best way to avoid getting into too much credit card debt is to nip this mentality in the bud by keeping the credit limit manageable. Having too high a credit limit could be synonymous with "having a lot of money" for people whose money mindset is not as ideal as it should be.

For your credit limit, it would be best if it is equal to or lower than your *monthly* salary, never more than that. Why? This is to ensure that you literally cannot and do not spend above your means each month. If you are the type of person who still uses a combination of cash and credit card for your day-to-day purchases, then your credit card limit has to be lower than your monthly salary to make room for your usual cash purchases. Better yet, abandon the use of cash and charge everything to your credit card so it's easier to track your expenses. It's far safer to use a credit card than lugging around a huge amount of cash in your wallet or using your debit card – a big no! Using physical debit cards for point of sale or online transactions could expose its details to threat actors aiming to illegally withdraw money. Such fraudulent transactions can also happen to credit cards, but in my experience, it's easier to dispute such transactions and recover your credit than recovering your debit card funds.

What if your bank issues you a credit card with a limit that is higher than your monthly salary?

Call them up and request that your limit be reduced to your desired amount. Do not take no for an answer. If they say your limit is already at the minimum for that particular tier of card, and they cannot lower it, then ask them to change it to a lower tier credit card (i.e., from a mid-tier credit card to a starter or entry-level tier credit card). Lower tier credit cards do not usually have perks and privileges though, and if they do, those perks might not be any of the reasons (e.g., petrol rebates, cashback on groceries) why you signed up for that credit card in the first place. So, re-evaluate your priorities.

Let's take a look at the two scenarios below to practice on.

I really need the perks of this credit card. I already did my calculations, and the perks would definitely save me [insert amount here] for all my [insert type of purchase here]. I think it is worth keeping the credit card even if they cannot lower the limit anymore. I will just make sure I do not overspend and max it out.

Or:

I really cannot trust myself with this big a credit limit. It's so tempting. I can buy a lot of [insert your favourite thing to shop here] with that amount of credit limit. But I know I won't be able to pay it back with just this month's salary. And it might send me into a downward spiral of spending and debt. I guess it's okay to live without that [insert perks you are after for this credit card] and accept a lower tier credit card.

Decide accordingly.

If your negotiating efforts fall short and you cannot lower your credit card limit to equal to or less than your monthly salary, or if you decided whole-heartedly that you want to keep the credit card and just promise yourself to behave, then you might want to throw in this extra layer of protection for your own good: request a supplementary card.

A supplementary card's spending limit is within the primary card's limit, not on top of it. As the primary cardholder, you can set the maximum limit of your own supplementary card. For example, if your monthly salary is AED 25,000 (~USD 6,800) and you received a credit card with a limit of AED 40,000 (~USD 10,890), set up your supplementary card to have a limit of AED 25,000 (~USD 6,800) or less. Then cut up your primary credit card. That way, it will be as if your credit card limit is only AED 25,000 (~USD 6,800).

A cautionary note for those who plan to borrow money from the bank later on, either in the form of a personal loan, a car loan, or a mortgage: the bank takes into consideration any current liabilities you have before they lend you the money. What does this mean?

Let's say the bank you are borrowing money from assessed that you can borrow a maximum amount of 20x your monthly salary. Keeping our monthly salary example above, that means you can borrow a maximum of 20 x 25,000 = 500,000 (~USD 136,130). If you already have an existing car loan of AED 150,000 (~USD 40,830) in the same bank or from another financial institution, they will deduct the remaining liability of this car loan from your borrowing power. Even if you qualified for a half-a-million personal loan, they cannot give you that amount because they know you are also committed to paying the liability you incurred from your car loan. Our credit card limits are considered one of these liabilities. Even if you do not use your credit card at all, since it is an open line of credit, that amount is considered a liability.

Going back to the primary and supplementary cards we set up earlier with limits of AED 40,000 and 25,000 (~USD 10,890 and 6,800) respectively, keep in mind that even if you are using your supplementary card only (because you had cut up your primary credit card already), your considered liability for that line of credit is the credit card limit of your primary card. That means that for future loans, the higher your credit card limit is, the lower your borrowing power will be.

If your credit card is already from the entry-level tier and at its credit limit is at its lowest possible minimum and it's still not lower than your monthly salary, you have to re-evaluate if you really need this credit card. Do not ever think that, *"If the credit card company gave me this credit card, then I certainly deserve to use it!"* Banks and credit companies do *not* approve credit cards because they look out for *your* welfare. They approve them because each little plastic card serves as an income vehicle for them. With every transaction on a credit card, a portion of it goes to the creditors. They would definitely like to give you more opportunities for putting your expenses on your credit card because the more you use it, the more they earn from it.

In short, your credit limit is *not* a reflection of what *you* deserve as credit, but an invitation for you to spend more so *they* can earn more. Never ever consider your credit card limit as a status symbol. Having a credit card and a high credit limit do not make you instantly rich and wealthy.

Annual fees

Check the size of the annual fee to decide if it is worth keeping the card. Some credit cards have zero annual fee for your first year, then they will start charging anywhere between AED 250 to 450 (~USD 70 to 120) in the succeeding years.

I have never had a credit card that required annual fee payments, but I've read a lot of scenarios wherein the credit card owner requested for their annual fee to be waived. This can easily be done by calling your credit card issuer. You'll usually get a yes if you are a good and on-time payor and you are loyal and always abide by the terms of your credit card.

Another technique I've read about runs as follows: if the credit card issuer declines your request to have your annual fee waived, let them know you are cancelling the credit card because the annual fee does not justify you keeping the card. When you do this, make sure your card is fully paid at that time to add *gravitas* to your statement. If the credit card issuer values your patronage, they will usually decide to bend the rules your way to keep you as a client, and a satisfied one at that.

Cancel any credit card that has an annual fee and has no perks right away. Although this is quite rare, it goes without saying that this is a no-brainer decision.

If you really must keep a card that incurs you an annual credit card fee, make sure the perks you get from it will break even, or better yet be higher than the cost of its annual fee. Let us look at some scenarios that will put this principle into practice.

Imagine you are to receive two different credit cards with the following benefits, but you only need one. Or, better yet, you *must* own only one. Which one would you keep?

Credit card A has an annual fee of AED 250 (~USD 70) and one of the perks is a 10% monthly cashback for all your petrol purchases, capped at AED 100 (~USD 30). Suppose you spend AED 800 (~USD 220) per month for petrol. If you put all your petrol purchases to this credit card, a 10% cashback each month means you will get AED 80 (~USD 20) back. If you multiply this to 12 months, you will approximately receive a total annual cashback of AED 960 (~USD 260) just from your petrol purchases. Taking the annual fee from only this perk, you will be able to save at least AED 710 (~USD 190) by just using this card. If it has other perks like cinema discounts or free airport lounge access, there is no doubt you have more than broken even.

Or:

Credit card B, with its AED 450 (~USD 120) annual fee, has a monthly grocery cashback of 2% capped at AED 200 (~USD 50). If you spend AED 1,000 (~USD 270) per month for groceries, a 2% cashback means you gain AED 20 (~USD 5) back each month. AED 20 x 12 months = AED 240 (~USD 70). With an annual fee of AED 450 (~USD 120), you are not breaking even at all. Look up the other perks of this credit card to see if you can justify paying the annual fee. If not, then you know what the answer is to the question above.

Remember, this is an oversimplified example of how you can decide if a credit card is worth keeping or not. Decide as you see fit.

A more aggressive antidote

If you feel like the above antidote is not enough to protect you against overspending, then set your credit card limit to an amount equivalent to your disposable income minus the amount you want to save each month, rent and recurring monthly payables.

To compute for this amount, use the formula below:

Monthly salary − (intended savings + rent/mortgage + electricity + water + mobile + home internet/cable/landline + transport/car repayment + optional: monthly instalments for any loan you might have) = credit card limit

Example: AED 15,000 − (3,000 + 3,000 + 500 + 100 + 300 + 300 + 800 + 2,000) = AED 5,000 is left

If your monthly salary is AED 15,000 (~USD 4,080) and you take out a total of AED 10,000 (~USD 2,720) for all your fixed monthly expenses, then your credit card limit should only be AED 5,000 (~USD 1,360). This way, the credit card limit can only accommodate the amount you would usually spend on food and other "non-fixed" expenses. You may not need to use your credit card for these expenses because based on our calculation above, you have enough money left from your monthly salary to cover for these. However, if you do decide to put your non-fixed expenses to your credit card, do so only if:

(1) you want to use your credit card instead of your debit card for security and practical reasons, or

(2) charging these items will accrue points for your credit card reward system.

Regardless, the reason should *never* be because you do not have the money for the purchase. Also, you must pay the outstanding amount down to zero by the end of your credit card's billing cycle. Remember again that from the example above, you still have enough money left from your monthly salary to pay for whatever you purchased with your credit card this month.

If your credit card has a rewards system that grant points for every purchase you make, you might want to charge your electricity, water, mobile and transport bills to it as well. Your credit card limit will need to be higher, but you'll still have enough cash left to make sure you can fully pay your total amount by the end of the billing cycle. Your formula will then be something like this:

Monthly salary – (intended savings + rent/mortgage) = credit card limit

Example: AED 15,000 – (3,000 + 3,000) = AED 9,000 is left

With that higher credit card limit of AED 9,000 (~USD 2,450), you can now pay for your utility bills using your credit card. You then earn points, miles, or rebates for these charges. Pay off the amount in full within each billing cycle so you do not accumulate any finance charges.

With my ignorance about credit card use back then, I definitely set myself back years of lost wealth-building opportunities. You could easily say, *"It's okay, just charge it to experience,"* to pacify me, but what happened was it all got "charged" to my credit card, at a very pricey interest rate!

HOW DID I GET RID OF MY CONSUMER DEBTS?

You don't need to read any book, take any course, or pay for an expert's advice to know how to get rid of debt. Common sense dictates that we need more money (surplus) to pay down debt (scarcity). But where do we get *more* money? This is the more usual and valid question.

Time and time again, we'd hear people say, *"Make a budget!"* But the flaw in this plan is that we can only cut costs down to a certain point. *Earning more*, however – whether through asking for a salary raise or working a side hustle or starting a business – has no limit, which makes it a more viable option to pay down debt faster. Imagine what the combination of making a budget and earning more could do to your financial health.

Getting rid of all my consumer debts was a happy by-product of my move overseas. I didn't deliberately seek to be instantly debt-free, despite my realisation of how hard it is to get up in the morning just to go to work. But I suddenly found myself in a situation wherein I could be debt-free. As soon as I found employment in Abu Dhabi, I was able to pay off all my credit card debts in the Philippines with my first month's salary. I was elated! The feeling of doom from my accumulated consumer debts in the Philippines was instantly gone. Being debt-free was quite exhilarating! And that feeling made me want to educate myself more about personal finance.

In Abu Dhabi, I worked for a government-owned institution from 2013 to 2022. This made it easier for me to establish a good credit history with my bank. In the UAE, unlike in the United States and most countries, banks and creditors do not necessarily rely on a credit score system to open a credit line for you or to lend you money. They do have a credit bureau, but back in the early 2010s, we residents did not necessarily have a credit score that we needed to actively keep up or improve so we could borrow a good amount of money. They simply looked at our monthly salary and who our employer was and presto, they already had a number in mind for us. This was how I received two credit cards (a Visa and a Mastercard) with AED 20,000 (~USD 5,450) limit each within days of my arrival.

It happened when I opened a bank account where my salary would be deposited each month. I didn't even have to go to the bank to do this. On my first day at work, I was in the HR office for my orientation, and there was a guy from the bank sitting across from me. The HR staff introduced him as one of the employees of the bank they usually recommended to new staff. I filled in the application form right there and then and within a day, my bank account was already up and running.

I expected to receive an ATM card by mail, so I could withdraw money the usual way, instead of going to the bank, filling up a withdrawal slip, queueing up to the teller, and withdrawing money over the counter. However, when I received the bank's mail, I didn't only receive a debit card, I also received a cheque book, and the two pre-approved credit cards, which I mentioned above.

When banks see you have a generous salary from a stable employer (who could be more stable than the government itself?), they see those as signs of having good credit, so they are happy to give credit cards or personal loans in a jiffy. In reality, it means you are most likely not to miss out on payments because your employer has an excellent reputation of paying salaries on time. Having a good enough salary also does not hurt.

In the UAE, employers pay the salary in full once a month. Yes. You read that right! Once a month, usually at the end of the month. But I have heard of a few private companies that pay their employees anytime during the first week of the month or the middle of the month. Regardless, the pay is given once in full amount, for the work provided in the previous four weeks. This was such a challenge for me as I was so used to receiving pay every two weeks back in the Philippines. But, at that time, I had no idea that this once-a-month pay was actually a game changer for the better!

The other thing about income in the UAE is, and you have probably heard this from someone you know, employee income is tax-free. Another game changer for me. I didn't have to think about tax deductions, income tax returns, and such.

Apparently, receiving my full income once a month made it much easier to manage my finances. At that point, I was dead set on taking my personal finances seriously. My sister, who at that time had been living in Dubai for almost a decade, sent me a budgeting spreadsheet she had been using to track her and my brother-in-law's finances.

I instantly fell in love with how neat and organised everything was. She made a category for everything. Each main expense category occupied one row. Each column showed the month of the year. All functions were put in, so all I needed to do was enter the values applicable to me and it would automatically compute how much I would have left at the end of each month after expenses, or how much I could save for a year.

I never knew putting all my numbers in one place could give me such invaluable insight. Seeing all the possible investment endeavours I could take with the money I could earn gave me an awakening jolt. This was when I finally decided I would never ever end up having to play catch-up again with my consumer debts. Simply put, my purchases had to be mindful, and they had to be paid down to zero come salary day.

In keeping up with my plan to never be immersed in consumer

debt anymore, I only activated one of the two credit cards my bank had given me. Activating both meant I'd have had a total of AED 40,000 (~USD 10,890) of liabilities right away, and that was scary for me. I trusted myself but I did not trust threat actors out there who would do anything to put enormous fraudulent transactions onto anyone's credit card. I did have credit insurance though, but why take the risk when I did not need two credit cards at all? In hindsight, I should have had the other credit card completely closed rather than keeping it "just in case" I needed more credit. Moreover, keeping both credit cards was in violation of my other credit card principle of keeping my credit limit to an amount equal to or less than my monthly salary. Having only one was more in keeping with this principle.

I learned to travel more during my time in Abu Dhabi. Instead of going back to the Philippines during my annual leave, I flew to other countries to see more of the world and learn more. At that point, I did not have a sinking funds system yet (more on this in a later chapter), so whenever I travelled, I used my credit card for all my expenses, and then paid it all off using my savings. In hindsight, it was not the best and most cost-efficient way to use my savings, but at least I did not have any outstanding debts. Not once did I ever max out my credit card. That was totally true, until I met my partner. Who knew dating could be so expensive?

MAXED-OUT CREDIT CARDS

In 2016, I remember asking a friend, *"Do you ever feel like you are living your life on the edge?"* I sometimes ask these kinds of questions when I want to feel like I'm not alone in fighting a certain battle in my life. If I hear that one of my contemporaries is experiencing the same fight as me, it quells my anxiety, and my panic goes away. It certainly is true that there is courage in numbers.

But what does this question of living life on the edge have to do with credit cards? An idiomatic expression, living on the edge means living a risky or dangerous lifestyle and accepting its consequences and the distress it brings. Maxing out my two credit cards was my proverbial *living on the edge* feeling, except that I never wanted to accept its possible consequences (i.e., crippling debt, poor credit history), and I never felt peaceful in the distress it brought.

What happened was, two years after eradicating my consumer debts from all those years of overspending, I entered my overspending *phase II* that led to two maxed-out credit cards. The only difference this time was that I could pay off my credit cards in full every month as compared to my overspending *phase I* when it snowballed into massive debts. Technically, I wasn't in debt during my overspending *phase II*, but I also wasn't saving any money.

What precipitated this situation of maxing out my credit cards was meeting my partner. I don't mean he spent all my money and maxed out my credit cards. Here, let me paint you a picture. Do you remember what it was like during the early days, weeks, months and years of your new relationship? Did you not want to always spend time with your new partner? Do activities with them? Travel everywhere with them? Give them gifts even when it isn't a special occasion? For me, it felt like we had missed each other for the first three decades of our lives (we were both in our 30s when we met each other) and we were trying so hard to catch up in order to make up for lost time.

We've established earlier that I love eating out, but he wasn't much of a foodie prior to our meeting, which led me to wanting him to try out all the restaurants I had been to, and all my favourite cuisines and dishes. But eating out once a day was not enough. So, we dined out every chance we got, such that breakfast, lunch and dinner were eaten at restaurants and buffet brunches.

He also wasn't much into travelling before we met, so I introduced him to the world of short and long trips that were neither in the Philippines nor in the UAE. We started taking week-long trips during our first year together and month-long trips right around the second-year mark. He immediately took to enjoying driving around the countryside, be it in a country with right-hand (what we are used to) or left-hand traffic. Car rentals and hotels have always been the biggest chunk of our expenses when we travel. But food is what we enjoy the most (even more than visiting museums). Sometimes, our travel would also include shows, musicals, concerts and antiquing. And those activities drive up the cost of our trips.

At the same time as I introduced him to eating out and travelling, he introduced me to different outdoor adventures. Between the two of us, he is the more outdoorsy one. I felt I had finally met the person who would push me to ultimately try out all the activities and experiences on my bucket list. Things I wanted to do but hesitated to try because (1) I didn't have any friends interested in the same things, (2) I was afraid to do them on my own, and (3) they were too costly, so I had to pace myself in doing them.

For example, I had always wished to get a PADI open water scuba diving certification. It had been on my bucket list ever since I saw the seas of Puerto Galera and Boracay when I was younger. Snorkelling didn't cut it and the view from such shallow depths did not do justice to the beauty of the underwater world.

When I started earning, I thought of finally getting my PADI certification, but I kept delaying it because, as I have mentioned earlier, my personal finances were quite chaotic upon my entry to the workforce. There was not enough time and money for leisure and things like a PADI scuba diving certification.

When I moved to the UAE, the extra time after work allowed me to re-explore my almost forgotten bucket list of activities. The work-life balance in the UAE was a thousand times better than my brief time in the Philippine workforce. There was too much time to be filled, too much fun to be had and too many thrills to be sought. So, I went and did most of it.

Being a certified scuba diver meant doing dives every chance we got, mostly during weekends or short holidays. That entailed renting a boat to take us off the coast so we could access beautiful dive sites. Or joining dive tours in nearby countries. No matter the mode, they all cost money. On top of that, because he was a certified PADI instructor when I met him, it meant he knew all the most reliable gadgets for scuba diving, which also meant he recommended I used them, from dive computer to regulator to suits.

Meeting him also led me to purchasing my very first time-trial bike for triathlon events. Prior to meeting him, I was always just the swimmer in a triathlon relay. He pushed me to train for all three disciplines so I could finally complete the whole event. We both joined in triathlon races too and we each had our own equipment for swimming, cycling and running.

He also has a penchant for hiking, trekking, trail walking and camping and he was the one who taught me to dress properly for all outdoor occasions and activities. Prior to meeting him, I had always had a mindset of *pwede na yan* (that will do), like most of our *kabayans* (fellow countrymen). I remember trail walking in Cappadocia in my leather ankle boots that were meant for city walks, because in my head, that pair would do. Nothing bad happened to me, but I cannot deny that the walk in the mountains would have been more comfortable if I had been wearing the right type of shoes. After meeting my partner, I learned from him the importance of wearing the right shoes (and clothes) for the activity and not skimping on them, because it is my body that they are protecting.

I could not be more right in assuming these things and activities do cost a lot of money. So, can you imagine me finally having the courage to do all these adventures with him one weekend after another? Every adventure required different tools, equipment, gadgets and outfits. Can you imagine what that meant for my budget?

On top of this, we gave each other expensive gifts on special occasions and even on ordinary days, as if we were compensating for all the years that we were not able to give gifts to each other prior to meeting. Let's just say that the concept of budgeting was virtually non-existent during those early years of our relationship.

For our hobbies and trips, we always paid 50-50 for everything. A gentleman would always insist he pays for the woman, and he did insist. But I was adamant that I paid for my own expenses. I had my own income and I insisted on not being a burden on somebody else's finances. At that point, we were charging everything to my credit card and paying off everything at the end of the month, 50-50. We were technically not in debt because we paid off every single dirham we owed each month, but it also meant we didn't have any savings during those first few years of being together. And that led me to feeling a bit uneasy.

I was happy to be collecting all those new memories with him and going on adventures. I've always been an avid fan of collecting memories instead of things. But at the back of my mind, while we spent almost all our earnings on adventure, food trips, travel and everything else, maxing out our credit cards felt like I was living life on the edge because should anything happen to me or should I lose my job while not having any money cushion, I was sure to suffer.

My only saving grace and comfort at that time was the belief that as long as I kept working, I would be fine. Haven't you had similar inner thoughts too? Sometimes though, such a situation builds a feeling of resentment towards your job during seasons of heightened busyness and toxicity at work, but you know you have to stay because you have a lifestyle to fund. That setup breeds animosity towards a job you used to like, until you start to hate having to go to work.

In contrast to me, my partner was not affected by our overspending. To this day, he does not mind spending everything he has on the things and experiences he likes. We are opposites when it comes to personal finance. I always worry for the future; he always wants to live life to the fullest now. I'm not comfortable without savings, while he is fine without them as long as he keeps working. I'm comfortable with delaying gratification, while he needs enrichment on a constant basis.

Despite us being complete opposites, he recognises and respects the fact that I will go crazy without the safety net that savings and emergency funds provide. So, three years into our relationship, we decided to rein in our overspending. It was around the same time we felt like we had finally "caught up" with each other's hobbies. We started streamlining our spending on things and hobbies we both liked and were rejuvenating for both of us. We each have separate hobbies as well, and we still constantly go on dates. As of writing, our hobbies and dinners out are very well curated, and we do not need to max out our credit cards to do all of them.

I think the lessons I want to drive home here are two-fold. First, new relationships are expensive. While there are more economical and less bank-breaking ways to spend your time together getting to know each other during the earlier stages of your relationship, chances are you will still spend an amount of money that you would not normally spend if you were single or if you have been in a relationship for quite some time now. So, to those who are currently single and are about to enter the dating world, brace yourselves and your pockets! Make sure you have enough for it, and in the likely event that you might overspend, make sure the memories are all worth it.

The second lesson is that you can bring your individual money ideology into your relationship, but you do not have to impose it on each other. There is no reason for you to fight over whose personal finance practices prevail. There is also no reason to just conform to what is already a common practice of couples in society. Just do what is most comfortable for the both of you.

Right now, we manage our money separately. We still pay for everything in a 50-50 split. We still give each other expensive gifts, but mostly towards experiences rather than gadgets because we learned it was so hard to let go of an old device that the other had gifted. We have agreed that if we gift an experience to each other instead of the latest gadgets, there will be no need to decide whether to keep the "junk" or give it away.

Antidote to a crippling debt due to maxed-out credit cards

Always aim for zero as the outstanding balance every time your credit card statement is generated. Yes, you read that right. Zero.

Now, I know this may sound counter-intuitive given that I have been encouraging you to use your credit card since the start of this chapter, albeit wisely. But what this means is you need to pay off your card in full every time you use it.

There's no telling how deep your debt could go if you miss one full payment and you let it snowball. Remember, the only two acceptable reasons why we are using our credit card are: (1) we do not want to use our debit card for security and practical reasons, and (2) you want to make use of the perks of your credit cards either by way of accumulating points, cashback, discounts, etc. Not having the money required for the purchase is *not* a valid reason for using your credit card, especially if your aim is to achieve a debt-free life.

So, when is the right time to pay off the purchases you charged to your credit card? It is completely up to you. But here are four common options I have seen people choose:

1. **Pay your credit card after every purchase**. If you just bought a pair of shoes or a gadget that you have been eyeing and saving up for quite some time now, charge it to your credit card then transfer your saved money for this particular item onto the credit card. This way, you get to use the perk of your credit card, whatever it may be, without going into debt. This can be applicable too for other routine purchases like paying your bills, buying groceries, or filling up your car. Commonly, electric, water, cable, phone bills, etc. come on a monthly basis. In true debt-free fashion, if you have set aside part of your salary to pay for all these payables regardless of their billing dates, then it would not be hard paying and keeping your credit card down to zero not only every month, but each and every moment you own the card. If your phone bill comes every 15th of the month, pay it on the 15th using your credit card, then transfer to your credit card that same exact amount you just charged to your card to settle your phone bill. Do not wait up until the credit card bill is due. Do the same thing for your other recurring bills. If you choose this payment scheme, it will be tedious, but you will always have a completely paid for credit card.

2. **Pay your credit card weekly**. If you deem the first payment scheme above as too time-consuming for you, then pay for everything you charged to your credit card in one go at the end of each week, or on Mondays if you are gunning for the more symbolic *start your week right* feeling. If you already have a day of the week marked for your weekly budget check, you can also do your weekly credit card payment at that time, so everything related to personal finance is done in one sitting. This payment scheme will be beneficial for those people who receive their compensation weekly. Just remember to pay everything down to zero.

3. **Pay your credit card bi-weekly**. If your salary comes every

two weeks, then this payment scheme will coincide perfectly with your objective of paying your credit card down to zero.

4. **Pay your credit card monthly, right before the billing cycle**. The most common billing cycle of a credit card is every 30/31 days. If your credit card statement is generated on the 1st day of each month, aim to pay it fully on the 28th, 29th, 30th, or 31st of the month, depending on which month it is at the time of payment. As soon as you receive your credit card statement on the first of the new month, your outstanding balance should read AED 0.00. This is my preferred payment method. I have a credit card that starts its cycle from the sixth of the month to the fifth of the next month. I make sure I pay it fully on the 5th of every month. There is a different kind of high that comes from seeing my credit card showing zero outstanding balance every time I receive the statement via email. It facilitates that feeling of *"I do not owe anyone anything,"* and, *"It is good to actually own and not owe everything that I have right now."* Another advantage of this payment scheme is that, if you have followed my recommendations about finding your ideal credit limit, you will have just the right amount of room to charge for everything you need in a month, which conversely becomes a disadvantage of paying it prior to the end of your billing cycle, like the first three payment schemes I mentioned above.

For example, on a credit limit of AED 10,000 (~USD 2,720), if you use up AED 2,500 (~USD 680) on the first week of the month and you try to pay if off weekly, by the start of your second week, you again have a *credit space* of AED 10,000 (~USD 2,720). If you are not careful with your budgeting, this might give you a false sense of purchasing power. Every time you pay off your credit card, whether it is after every purchase, weekly, or bi-weekly, it creates an inflated credit in your mind. You always think you are entitled to that AED 10,000 (~USD 2,720), but that is only if you are not careful with your budgeting.

This is why it is important for you to have a routine schedule for checking on your monthly budget. It does not have to be daily and long, but it has to be frequent enough to keep you tethered to your realistic budget, so you do not overspend through your inflated credit space. This also applies the other way around. Checking your budget at reasonable intervals can also prevent underspending. You might already be depriving yourself without realising it, despite having the means and purchasing power. Remember, being and keeping debt-free will only be worth it if you are happy and you do not feel deprived.

Another good thing about this payment scheme is that it works well with people who receive their income weekly, bi-weekly, or monthly. You might even earn yourself a few extra bucks by keeping your money earmarked for credit card payment in a high yield savings account while waiting for the last day of your billing cycle to pay it off. Some banks allow you to open an e-savings account that pays off interest and does not require a minimum balance to be maintained. This is what I used to keep my *credit card payment money* so I would not be tempted to withdraw it until the time I needed it to pay my credit card fully. More about high yield savings and e-saver accounts in a future chapter.

CLOSING MULTIPLE CREDIT CARD DEBTS

As I mentioned at the beginning of this chapter, I've only ever had a maximum of two credit cards at a time. I do, however, know some people who have multiple credit cards. Some are maxed out, others are almost maxed out. Some of them have been wanting to close all their credit cards or some of them just to alleviate the strain of debt, while others are still applying for more credit cards.

I've always wondered what I would do if I were trapped in multiple credit card debts. So, I started reading what others have done. Two popular schemes always pop up in my readings: the avalanche method and the snowball method.

1. **Avalanche method.** With this method, you arrange your credit cards from highest to lowest interest rate. The card with the highest interest rate is the top priority to be paid off

and closed right away as the high interest rate compounds the amount owed over time.

2. **Snowball method.** With this method, you arrange your credit card from lowest to highest outstanding balance. The aim is to close the credit card with the lowest balance first. This method relies on the fact that aiming for a small goal and achieving it right away provides a surge of excitement and the necessary push to make you want to hit your next goal as soon as possible. It helps you feel that your debt repayment goals are realistic and achievable.

Keep in mind that in both methods above, you keep on paying the minimum amount due on the other cards while you pay *more* than the minimum amount due on the first credit card you aim to close, whether it's the one with the highest interest rate (avalanche method) or the one with the lowest outstanding balance (snowball method).

Once you completely pay off the first credit card, cancel it right away. The money you used to pay for it will then be redirected to paying the second credit card in line. Repeat the process until you have paid all your credit card debts down to the last one.

Assuming you have five credit cards and you want to close them all, let's use the following hypothetical example to decide how to proceed.

Table 1. Sample details of five credit cards you want to pay off and close

Credit card	Credit limit	Interest rate	Outstanding balance
A	5,000	15%	4,721
B	7,000	19.99%	5,089
C	6,000	16.5%	5,725
D	5,000	22%	1,899
E	5,000	24%	4,955

With the avalanche method, the very high interest rate of credit card E makes it the first priority to be paid off, followed by credit cards D, B, C and A.

With the snowball method, the low outstanding balance of credit card D becomes top priority, followed by credit cards A, E, B and C.

Remember, as you close the first credit card, extra payments will now go to the second credit card in line, with the rest still receiving minimum payments.

If you do decide to keep one credit card for daily use, it *should* be paid down to zero every billing cycle.

SHOULD YOU USE THE CASH ADVANCE FEATURE OF YOUR CREDIT CARD?

The only acceptable answer to this question is no. To reiterate, credit cards are *not* for emergency purposes. The cost doesn't justify the borrowing.

I remember the only time I ever withdrew cash from my credit card was because I got backed into a corner by someone who lent me money which I didn't expect she needed back so soon. It was during a time when the construction of my building was ongoing (more on this later), and somewhere along the way, I needed to add funding. The amount wasn't too big that it required another loan (AED 10,000 or ~USD 2,720), but I needed to wait for my next salary to come before I could send the money home.

My friend offered to lend me the said amount just when I needed it, and I promised to pay her back as soon as my next salary came in, which was only two weeks away. I've always been uncomfortable borrowing money from friends, but I grabbed her offer because it was a timely one. I also thought she wouldn't make a fuss about it since she was the one who made the offer and I'd done the same favour for her before by lending her money a couple of times with amounts way bigger than what I needed at that time, at no extra cost and no due date against her. But ten days into the deal, she wanted me to pay up already. As I said, I'm not comfortable borrowing money from friends so I paid her back right away as soon as she demanded the money, no questions asked, even if she had reneged on our original deal. And since my salary hadn't come yet at that time, I resorted to taking the amount from my credit card, which came with a hefty price tag.

There was a transaction fee at a flat rate of AED 250 (~USD 70), plus the interest of 12% on the borrowed amount that started on the day I took out the cash. I felt horrible for paying service fees when I could have waited for my salary at no extra cost to me.

If there's another lesson we can take away from this scenario on top of learning to never take cash advances from credit cards, it is to never be naïve about the terms and conditions of borrowing money, be it from your friends, relatives or from financial institutions. Let's talk more about borrowing money in the next chapter.

CHAPTER 3
ON BORROWING MONEY

One fine day, I received a call from a loan agent from one of the biggest banks in the UAE. He started pitching their personal loan offers and how low their interest rates are. I politely declined his offer and told him I did not have any need for such a loan at that moment. I even mentioned I would save his direct line so if the time came when I did need a loan, I would make a call straight to his number. He didn't let me go right away. He was determined to get me hooked and sign me up for a personal loan, probably seeing in his system that: (1) my salary made me eligible to borrow a huge amount, (2) I was employed by the government, and (3) I did not have any current personal loans – the trifecta of a perfect loan candidate. Sometimes, I hate myself for being over-polite especially on phone calls: once I pick up a call, I do not hang up unless both parties have said their goodbyes. I tried telling him once again that I was not interested and here was how the rest of our conversation went:

Me: It's okay. Thank you for your offer, but I don't really need a loan right now.

Loan agent: But you cannot pass up this offer! The interest rate is very low!

Me: No, it's okay. I really don't need it. I will hang up now.

Loan agent: Why don't you take a loan and keep the cash in your bank. You can use it for your lifestyle. That's what I and my family do. We take a loan in January for a 12-month term, spend the money for shopping and stuff, and we just pay it off each month for the rest of the year.

Did your jaw drop too? Even I couldn't believe that this person, who works in the banking industry, would advocate getting a loan so I could use it for *shopping and stuff*. Getting a personal loan to fund your lifestyle is like the worst kind of debt you can get yourself into. I cannot think of anything worse. But of course, I should not have expected any altruistic motive from a loan agent since he was only doing his job. As I said in an earlier chapter: "Banks and credit companies do *not* approve credit cards because they look out for *your* welfare. They approve them because each little plastic card serves as an income vehicle for them."

Similarly, each approved personal loan will earn (1) a commission for the agent and (2) interest payments for the bank or creditor. That's why that loan agent was determined to sign me up for a loan even when I explicitly said I had no need for one. He wasn't doing that out of the goodness of his heart. He wasn't doing that to solve a dire money situation I was in, or to help me achieve my dreams (e.g., purchase an existing business, put a deposit on my dream home, etc.). He was doing that as part of his job regardless of whether my going into debt would be good for my well-being or not. So, be very careful not to take predatory loans like that!

PERSONAL LOANS

As I have mentioned in the section introduction and first chapter of this book, loans – and debt, for that matter – are not inherently bad. In fact, if you plan to acquire an asset and invest in something that is income generating (e.g., as capital for your business; to buy shares in the stock market), then taking a personal loan might even hasten the fulfilment of your plan. But if you intend to spend it to fund your life-style – like how the sneaky loan agent above tried to sell to me – or any endeavour that will not generate dividends and income, then that loan could be a recipe for personal financial disaster. In short, depending on where you put the money you borrowed, loans could either make or break your finances.

Think of a personal loan as enforced saving. This would be advantageous for people who always have trouble keeping their hands off their savings. You always hear them say, *"I could never save. If I see I have money in my bank account, I'm always tempted to spend it."* I totally understand them. But that mindset is counter-intuitive if they are trying to save up for *something big*. They will always end up going back to square one.

To prevent that from happening, it is better to take a personal loan, buy that *something big* and let the bank automatically take the money out of their account as soon as their salary comes in. But, you ask, what about the interest? You might think, it is a waste of interest fee when they could simply change their mindset about saving or keeping the saved-up money out of sight, so they are not tempted to touch it. While you are not wrong, it is almost always easier said than done. So, for them, it would be better to see the interest fee as a *service charge*, a token of appreciation for helping them *forcefully* save money so they can finally acquire their *something big*.

Personal loans can also catapult your entrepreneurial goals from dream into reality. If it will take a lot of time to save up for your capital and you deem that the profit of starting the business now outweighs the interest fee of borrowing money, then it is better to take a loan now and start that business right away. This is what I did with my apartment building in my hometown. I took a personal loan from my salaried bank account in the UAE payable in four years, then I had the building built within a year. This meant that on the second year of paying my loan, my building was already up and generating income. I didn't have to wait for months or years to accumulate a good sum of money to start putting in the first foundations of my building, thanks to that personal loan. So, when you take a personal loan, make sure you have a genuine need for it, not just a fleeting one. It's also a good thing to consider not taking a loan while in a job that you hate. It could be a catastrophic disaster for your mental health if you feel like you need to stay in your crappy job just to pay off your loan.

At the start of your personal loan, your agent might offer you the opportunity to defer the first month of payment and you might glee-fully agree to it without any hesitation. Your agent might even float the idea that you can defer your payment any time should you need to be cash-rich during a specific calendar month (e.g., you're about to travel overseas or your kid's tuition fee is due soon). But any deferment, whether at the start or during the tenure of your loan, increases your unpaid amount because interest could still accrue during the month or months you choose to defer payment. Deferment doesn't necessarily just delay the whole payment schedule to a month later, it also compounds the interest on the outstanding balance, and therefore increases the total amount of the loan. But they don't explicitly tell you this, especially if you don't ask, *"What's the catch?"* So, if you're the type who doesn't read the terms of your loan, chances are you might be blindly deferring your loan payments every now and then without any regard to the consequences. Remember, it's never free money during the months that you defer. Think of the bigger picture: your total loan amount at the end of it all.

Do not take personal loans for travelling or once-in-a-lifetime experiences

You might say, *"But wait, we thought you are an advocate of collecting memories instead of things? Why are you against borrowing money to pay for experiences which will make lasting memories?"*

Personal loans are categorised as unsecured loans because they don't require any collateral to allow the lending of money from an institution to an individual. You can only borrow an amount lower than what you can borrow with a mortgage – where a house is at stake – or a car loan, where a car serves as collateral. If, for any reason, you suddenly are unable to pay your mortgage or car loan (the usual is defaulting payment for at least 90 days or, in short, three missed monthly payments), the bank will take what they are owed through your house (foreclosure) or your car (repossession), respectively.

With personal loans, the bank doesn't own anything to secure their stake in the transaction, and if you do spend what you borrowed for travel or an activity or anything non-tangible, you also wouldn't have any assurance that you can settle your debt should you lose the ability to pay them back. They do have insurance for it though and you pay for that insurance on top of your loan premium and interest (usually at 1% of the loan amount). Yes, that insurance you are paying for is not for *you* if you cannot pay the loan anymore. It is an assurance for the bank if you cannot pay them anymore.

What if you can't pay your personal loan anymore?

More often than not, our ability to pay back our personal loan is tied to our salary from our jobs. In the UAE, the Central Bank is strict on imposing that each borrower's equated monthly instalment (EMI) for their loan and liabilities be pegged at no more than half of the borrower's monthly salary. This is to ensure that each borrower's debt-burden ratio (DBR) is kept at a realistic level, without sacrificing their standard of living and to avoid financial hardship due to high liability). If you lose your job, your ability to pay your loan's EMI goes with your job. The ideal thing to do is to find another job, right? That is indeed the ideal thing to do.

What if you cannot find a job right away? What are you going to do when you suddenly can't pay for your loan anymore? Run away? You wouldn't have to run away in the first place if you were wise enough to have invested your borrowed money to acquire an asset, build a business, or used it to generate more income. You could try any one of these possible remedies, whichever you think might work for your situation:

- If your investments can generate enough income to be able to pay back the EMI, problem solved!
- Ask for deferment – but this doesn't really solve the

problem, it just delays and prolongs the problem and balloons the interest payment at the end of it all.

- If you find a job but it's outside the country of debt and you're on a travel ban list because of the unpaid loan, try to renegotiate with your bank and come up with an agreement on how you can settle your loan remotely. This might involve taking legal advice if necessary. The travel ban can only be lifted if both parties – meaning you and the creditor – reach an accord that is beneficial to both of you.

- If none of the above works, the worst-case scenario is to sell the asset or business and use the sales to pay for your loan. If it had happened to me, I would have sold my apartment building at home and used the sales to pay off my personal loan in the UAE. Another option for me would have been to take out a personal loan back at home with my building as collateral and used that money to pay off my loan in the UAE. In the latter option, I would lose a lot in the exchange rate, and I wouldn't have eliminated my debt, but at least I'd still have my building and it would continue to generate income for me, which I could use to pay off my debt in the Philippines.

You see, there are a lot of options available. This is not even a comprehensive list. And if you're ever in this situation, never run away from your payment obligations because you might think you have outsmarted the bank by escaping from your debt, but such an act would go on your record. Do not take it lightly!

———

Speaking of running away, when I came to Abu Dhabi in 2013, I was surprised to hear of stories about people who took out personal loans and absconded from their employment afterwards. What typically happens is, an individual who has been employed for at least a year or so, takes a personal loan from their bank. When they travel out of the UAE for their annual vacation leave or holidays, they never come back! Quite sinister, right? I was intrigued with the psychology of such people and of course, their ability to sleep at night knowing they had done something disturbing. I'm assuming their internal dialogue would have been along the lines of any one of these:

*"It's just a small sum of money compared to what that bank
    earns."*
*"The Central Bank, and in turn, the government, will not miss
    that money."*
*"They have insurance to recoup what I took. And I paid for
    that insurance!"*

And unfortunately, it happens more often than you might expect, and not just in places or industries where you'd think people are extremely desperate to get *free* money. In my ten-year tenure in my Abu Dhabi employment alone, I heard of at least three colleagues (yes, lecturers as well!) who never returned for the new academic year. How much they owed their banks when they departed the country, I truly do not know. Some genuinely concerned peers even contacted them to do a wellness check, but they did a great job of getting themselves out of reach.

No matter what you do, *do not*, I repeat, do not take this route ever. It's not worth it. Why? Let us read through three real-life cases of how the repercussions of absconding from your financial obligations and debt in the UAE can inconvenience your life in the future. I have changed or hidden the names of the people involved to keep them unidentifiable.

Case 1

Ananda accumulated a lot of debt and defaulted on a lot of her payments, resulting in the authorities hounding her employer to give them Ananda's most recent contact details as they were sure she had been evading them. During that time, Ananda was taking her annual leave and was in her home country when the police talked to her employers to set up a way to talk to her and come up with a settlement agreement. One of Ananda's colleagues was worried for her because he knew that as soon as Ananda landed back on UAE soil, she would face the authorities, with a possibility of appearing in court to settle her liabilities. But Ananda didn't know that. And the police were monitoring all communication media with Ananda: her work email, her mobile, etc.

The concerned colleague couldn't possibly tell her about the setup because then the authorities would have known Ananda had been warned. They were expecting Ananda to fly back to the UAE after her annual leave was up and there would be no reason for her not to come back, unless someone had tipped her off about the entrapment.

On the day of her flight back to Dubai, out of desperation, her concerned colleague was able to warn her through a friend of a friend of a friend. Ananda cancelled her flight and didn't go back to the UAE. Of course, it was a happy ending for her, but not for the institutions she owed money to. And, as I said, even if you think you can outrun your debts, do consider the laws recognised internationally regarding debts. Can the UAE send people over to wherever you are to collect payments from you? Can they liaise with your current address' local banks to arrange a debt settlement agreement with you? It is out of the scope of this book to cover these specific details, but I do urge you to think it through.

Case 2

One day, a former colleague had to leave work early because she had to bail her cousin out of detention. She was so worried because the authorities gave her very scant details as to why her cousin had been detained and why they were contacting her.

Apparently, her cousin was flying from one of the gulf countries to southeast Asia, connecting through Dubai. Her cousin got picked up in Dubai International Airport and was brought by the authorities in Abu Dhabi, because of an outstanding debt from the Emirate of Abu Dhabi. My colleague had to settle the debt before her cousin could be released. The debt owed was from when the cousin was still working in the UAE. He left the UAE and moved on to work in another gulf country without settling his debt, which was just ~AED 16,000 (~USD 4,360). Do you think running away from this amount is truly worth the future inconvenience?

Case 3

In this case, the outstanding debt was with a former employer, not with a bank. A man had a connecting flight from New Zealand to Europe that required switching airplanes at Dubai International Airport. During the layover in Dubai, he got picked up by two policemen, escorted to Abu Dhabi and was dropped off at the HR department of his former employer, where he was asked to settle his outstanding liabilities.

The owed amount was actually for a housing benefit that the employer had paid for in advance for a year, which the man only lived in for a couple of months before absconding his employment six years prior to him being picked up during his layover at Dubai International Airport.

This case shows that no matter who you owe the money to, as long as they filed a complaint with the authorities, your name will be flagged at the immigration's database when you pass through passport control, even during connecting flights!

BORROWING MONEY FROM FRIENDS AND FAMILY

I borrowed money from friends during my earlier years studying in Manila whenever I found myself short of cash. This usually happened when friends suddenly wanted to go out after a long day at uni, to chill and hang out over food. I tended not to bring all my allowance in my wallet so normally, spur-of-the-moment outings like that rendered me short of cash. Nothing the next day's allowance couldn't fix.

Over the years, I've become wary of borrowing money from other people, especially when I started earning. I mentioned in the previous chapter about my mishap in accepting a friend's offer to lend me money, which I paid with a cash advance from my credit card. That experience fortified my resolve to never borrow money from others.

Call it being principled or just plain old ego, I can't sleep well when I owe anybody any amount of money.

On the other end of the spectrum, there are those who can sleep soundly at night despite mounds of chronic unpaid debt from friends and family, as if their friends and family owed them the money. What's even more amazing is that these people act as if they are the victims whenever the lender friend or relative asks for their money back. Borrowing from and lending money to friends and family can test relationships, especially if the borrower doesn't pay up as promised.

Do I lend money to friends and family? Truth be told, not always. First, there aren't many people who borrow money from me. I think they know I don't have any money to spare. :) All jokes aside, my friends and immediate family members are quite responsible with their finances, so, it's not often I encounter anyone who doesn't have a fund intended for use in times of emergency. I think in my entire adult life, I've only encountered one borrower every two years (usually from among my colleagues).

Second, I do lend money, but only when I have the means (spare cash). However, this is usually not the case, especially during times when I'm putting myself through school, putting up an investment, or filling up a sinking fund (more about this later) that's soon to be utilised. I say this to the borrower upfront (one of those rare moments when I become the opposite of a textbook people pleaser). Sometimes, I feel guilty for not being able to help with their cash emergency, but I always get reminded of that famous line we've all probably read before: *"A lack of planning on your part does not constitute an emergency on mine,"* and the guilt suddenly flies away.

Third, I'm a firm believer of the golden rule: if I don't bother or burden you with covering the gap in my financial needs, I expect you to do the same to me. It sounds harsh, but in the long run, it will protect our relationship with each other.

How much is enough to borrow/lend from/to friends and family?

For borrowers:

1. It's important to think ahead about the amount of money you're borrowing because it would determine if it should be borrowed from friends and family, or whether you need a financial institution to lend you that amount instead.

2. Remember, every working person you know has financial responsibilities of their own, and the amount you're borrowing from them most likely has been earmarked for something, no matter how small the amount is.

3. Always ask yourself, will the money I'm borrowing go to something that is worth borrowing for?

Example 1:

While living in a residential tower in Abu Dhabi, our flat was adjacent to that of a Filipino family who moved in three years after we did. We always saw the parents of the household along the corridors or while riding the lift, and we always gave a polite nod to each other. More than a year after they moved in, they came knocking on our door. My partner answered the door. The couple introduced themselves by their first name and asked to borrow AED 12,000 (~USD 3,260) which they needed to send to the Philippines for an emergency.

Based on the two principles above, I don't have to tell you that this couple got nothing from us that day. First, they failed to realise that the amount of money they were asking to borrow is better borrowed from financial institutions who can take that risk. Second, who puts in their budget a reserve of AED 12,000 under the category of *"just in case strangers need to borrow money from me?"*

Example 2:

A colleague asked to borrow AED 2,500 (~USD 680) from me. She didn't cite what the money was for. While the amount was something realistic enough to be borrowed from a friend or family member, the problem was that this person posted on her Facebook account that she had just bought the latest iPhone, and she wanted to buy one for her then boyfriend as well. The amount she wanted to borrow from me was exactly the price of the newly released iPhone at that time, and so she was borrowing that amount from whoever could lend her the money in order to buy a second iPhone to gift to her then boyfriend.

Based on the third principle above, going into debt for the latest trend (or to gift the latest trend) isn't the wisest thing to do financially. When I told her I didn't have the cash for it, she suggested I use my credit card for a cash advance, and she'd pay for the transaction fee and interest. Based on my cash advance story from the previous chapter, you already know I'm strongly against taking cash advances using credit cards. So, when another person sort of forces me to take one because I don't have enough cash to lend her and satisfy her keeping up with the latest trend, you can already infer whether she was able to borrow any money from me that day or not.

For lenders:

I learned the following from two people I look up to in life: *"Lend only the amount you are willing to part from."* That way, even if the borrower doesn't pay you back, you won't miss the money and you won't resent the borrower. When I first learned of this, I considered it a good guideline for how much money I'd be willing to lend.

However, as time went by, I became less and less a fan of it, not because I'm utterly selfish but because in general, we are all working hard in life. Some of us are blessed with a higher income than most, while some of us, just enough. Regardless of income, we are all working hard to get by in life. I don't see the point why other able-bodied adults like me would get a free pass when borrowing money, even if it's just a small amount. You might think I lack empathy or consideration, but I assure you, we are not helping someone in any way by letting them skate by their responsibilities.

In *The Millionaire Next Door*, Stanley and Danko described a concept called *"weakening of the weak"* where adult children who have been supported financially by their well-off parents every step of the way (e.g., college education, purchasing a house, putting up capital for their business, sending their kids to school) don't face any of the gritty demands of life, unlike their parents who had to work hard to achieve their wealthy status. Similarly, we are doing a disservice to our friends and family who repeatedly borrow money and don't pay up if we just shrug off the small amounts of money we are "willing" to lose. We need to help them pull themselves out of their debt cycle and we can't do that by constantly enabling them to borrow money from others without paying up.

If you know the borrower well, and you know they are a serial borrower who doesn't pay back their debt, weigh the importance of your relationship with them against the money you might lose if you decide to lend them the money. Consider which is more important. If you value your relationship highly, then it's better to establish boundaries about money and tell them upfront that you can't lend them any money. If you do this the very first time they try to borrow money from you, they are likely to understand and not bother you thereafter. But if you do lend them money twice or thrice followed by a no, they are likely to resent you for cutting them off. However, if you do continue to lend them money and you're not getting any of it back, you'd start to resent them. Your relationship would eventually turn sour and it's all because of money. So, if you really value your relationship with that friend or relative, it's best to establish boundaries right off the bat when it comes to lending money, and enforce it.

What does it mean when your friend or relative who borrowed money doesn't want to pay up and consistently evades you?

Common sense dictates that if someone who borrowed money from you doesn't pay you back, it simply means they don't have the means to pay you back. You would expect for them to work on their debt by perhaps working more hours, taking up a side hustle, etc. so they can have a surplus in their budget to pay up their lenders. But if their course of action is to hide and evade you at all costs, then they don't plan on paying you back at all.

What should you do?

Take a piece of paper and a pen. Write down the total amount they owe you. Stare at it intently, and tell yourself:

"This is the amount they sold our friendship/relationship for. They were willing to sacrifice our relationship to avoid paying up this amount of money. This was how much our relationship was worth in the end. If they were more willing to lose me than pay back this pathetic amount, then I guess it's good riddance."

Then don't expect the money back.

My partner, whom I've already mentioned in the previous chapter as very easy-going with his money, has lost a few family and friends this way. It's not because he started ignoring them when they didn't pay their debts to him, it's more because they stopped showing up. He doesn't hold any grudges towards them even if some of his cousins have intentionally conned him out of thousands of dirhams (he is that breezy when it comes to money). I guess at one point, they felt ashamed of what they did to him, which eventually led them to not show their faces, and then the relationship fell apart. Another example of how borrowing money from friends and family can ruin relationships!

I have only had one falling out with a relative when it comes to borrowed money. My distant uncle borrowed a huge sum of money from me in January 2015 to pay for his credit card debts, and I told him I needed the money back by July of the same year because the money was earmarked for my month-long trip to the USA. I told him he could pay me in instalments from February until June. He verbally agreed to the payment terms, but he never paid me a single dirham during those months, and I ended up using mostly my credit card for that trip.

When I came back from my US trip, I asked my aunt (his wife) if she could intervene getting my money from her husband because it was already long overdue. She was awfully shocked that her husband had borrowed such a huge amount of money from me. As it turned out, she wasn't aware of her husband's debt to me. She immediately paid me back 80% of it right on the spot. I appreciated her gesture and her promise that she would ask her husband to contact me and pay up the rest of his debt immediately. He never did reach out to me, and he never did pay back the rest of his debt. To this day, he has never spoken to me. The last time I saw him was that January when he picked up the money he borrowed from me. Prior to that, he and my aunt were regulars at brunches/dinners that I'd host at my home in Abu Dhabi, and we would sometimes dine out or watch movies together. Mind you, I didn't cut him out of my life because of his unpaid debt. I still frequented their place whenever my aunt would host dinners, and I still brought my parents to their place whenever they were in Abu Dhabi, but I never saw him in all those visits. He eventually moved back to the Philippines.

CAR LOANS

I never owned my own car in the UAE. I never really got around to completing my driving licence requirements. When I moved to the UAE in 2013, I immediately settled into the comfort of taking cabs everywhere. My first studio apartment was located in a villa within the city, where getting a public parking slot was cutthroat. I decided right off the bat that I didn't need that kind of stress in my life.

To go to work (which was located 36 km from where I lived), I paid for a monthly carpool service where a Toyota Coaster picked me up along with other hospital staff and employees from my workplace. The Toyota Coaster was actually a transport benefit provided to the staff of the hospital near the campus where I was working.

My workplace didn't provide that benefit. During my interview with them, it was suggested that having my own driving licence once hired would be a breeze. As I mentioned earlier, I got cosy with Abu Dhabi's public transport, and nobody could ever convince me to work on getting my driver's licence thereafter.

Some employees from my workplace didn't drive to work either. One of them even made a special arrangement with the transport company of the hospital nearby, possibly years before I first set foot in Abu Dhabi, to add a few of us on the roster of staff they had to pick up from the city. Of course, the hospital staff were their priority to drop off first, then off we went to the campus. After work, the driver would pick us up first, then head to the hospital to pick up the original service beneficiaries. This whole setup was so convenient for me because I could read a book in the morning and take a nap on the way back to the city in the afternoon.

Similarly, when I lived in Dubai for two years to be closer to my university where I was taking weekend classes for my PhD, I also carpooled to work on weekdays. I wasn't aware there were too many professionals working in Abu Dhabi but living in Dubai. It was usually a case of both husband and wife working but one was working in Dubai and the other in Abu Dhabi.

I never asked any of them why they chose to stay in Dubai instead of Abu Dhabi (introvert alert!) but I assumed it was one of the following three reasons. First, they probably settled in Dubai upon arriving in the UAE and when the other person lost or switched jobs, they might have found one in Abu Dhabi and decided to commute inter-state daily to keep their residence in Dubai. Second, similar to the first reason, add kids who already went to school in Dubai. Third, the one commuting every day from Dubai to Abu Dhabi and vice versa must have probably lost a coin toss.

So, there it is. In my decade-long stay in the UAE, as I mentioned earlier, I didn't own a car. But I remember almost buying one. Sometime in 2018, my partner and I went to a Toyota dealership. We started looking at their SUVs, particularly the Land Cruiser. At that time, my partner was driving a Nissan Patrol Safari, but all his UAE cars were provided by his employer. Beyond being a benefit, it was for security purposes, to ensure that all the cars that entered within the grounds of his workplace were owned and vetted by his employer.

Being in the UAE, we've become accustomed to outdoor activities such as camping in the desert and dune bashing. Of course, an SUV is a must in such situations. Hence, our constant pining for a Land Cruiser. To this day, I don't know why we had to buy a car at that time. I still couldn't justify it in my head why we wanted another SUV when he already drove one. I couldn't understand the need for another one that guzzled up petrol like there was no tomorrow. It's like wanting to buy another pair of shoes you don't need when you already have 400 pairs of them at home. I sure wasn't going to drive it to work anyway, I was completely comfortable napping and reading to and from work while carpooling.

The only thing I could remember from that time that compelled us to look for a car was that we were so bored during that season of our lives. We were stuck in a rut: work, spend, work, spend, work, spend. We were so out of touch with our life goals, and of the bigger picture, that we just went through each day without any North Star. And there we were, at a Toyota dealership, about to buy a car just for the hell of it.

We spoke with one of the car sales agents. He told us what documents we needed to submit for the financing and assured us he'd take care of everything. We went home, emailed the agent our usual identification documents (both our passports, Emirates ID, UAE residence visa) and financials (payslips, salary certificate). We waited to hear from him which bank we'd be using to finance the car, whether it was mine or my partner's (we had different banks back then).

Unfortunately (or fortunately), neither of us was eligible for car financing. It wasn't that we didn't have the money for it. We had the 20% down payment ready, and we had disposable incomes that were more than ten times the monthly instalment required, which meant we could easily cover the monthly repayments.

What was the problem then? We both had personal loans at that time. Remember, I said earlier that the Central Bank was strict on imposing that 50% of borrower's salary was their maximum EMI for all their liabilities with their bank. Each of us was paying 50% of our salary to pay off our personal loans at that time: the loan I took for the construction of my apartment building and my partner's loan for properties he bought in the Philippines. Both our banks couldn't give any more liability to either one of us even though, technically speaking, what was left of each of our salaries each month could finance at least ten more cars.

At that point, there were only two options for us:

1. We re-finance our personal loans to be paid at a longer tenure which would make our debt burden ratio lower than 50% of our salaries.
2. We borrow from a financial institution other than our banks. I'm not talking about shady financial institutions or loan sharks, but there usually are creditors that are more "flexible" in terms of the 50% EMI rule.

What did we end up doing to finally get our coveted Land Cruiser? Nothing. By the time we spoke to our agent again, our hankering for a Land Cruiser was gone. And it was just as well, because, as I said earlier, I really can't, for the love of me, figure out why we needed another car back then. And even if we really wanted to pursue the purchase, I wouldn't have done any of the two options above. Why? Because, at that time, I was six months away from paying off my personal loan in full. Why on earth would I want to spread it out over 12 or 24 more months of smaller payments, pay another loan agent's fee and insurance, just so I could accommodate another liability under my name? That's for the first option. And for the second one, I believe that the 50% EMI rule is there for a reason. It's not to stifle anyone from buying what they want in life. It serves as a safety net, and that safety net knocked some sense unto us. We were bitter for a good few minutes after not qualifying for car financing but brushed it off after a few more minutes of trying to understand why we really needed another SUV.

MORTGAGE

I'm in my late 30s as of writing and I've never had a mortgage in my life – yet. Is that a good thing? Not necessarily. That means I don't have a principal place of residence (PPOR).

I've been renting since I was 15 when I moved out of my parents' house to go to the capital of my home country and undertake my bachelor's degree. Of course, my parents paid for my rent while I was studying, then I started paying for it after finishing uni.

To date, I have had five lease contracts under my name, from

Manila to Abu Dhabi to Dubai and back to Abu Dhabi. It may be taxing to be moving around a lot and across cities and countries. But apart from my print books (then), board games and bikes (now), I don't own a lot of other huge things that would make moving a lot more inconvenient than it already is.

Still, it would be nice to have my (our) own permanent little place to live in or throw trinkets at from our travels. Whenever we'd go antiquing and we'd see something nice to keep, we'd always contemplate where we would put such a (delicate) piece. Then we'd abandon the idea because we knew that as long as we were in the UAE, we wouldn't have our permanent place and we'd be moving again soon.

Just to clarify, expats are allowed to buy and own properties in the UAE. In fact, a lot of my former colleagues have bought their own places in Abu Dhabi either as their primary residence or as an investment property. A colleague from a different department bought a property when she got hired at my workplace, and then sold it when she moved back to the UK after roughly three years. We are allowed to own, I just didn't buy.

Instead of taking out a mortgage, I took out a personal loan (as I mentioned earlier) and put up an apartment building in my hometown in the Philippines.

Why an apartment building and not my own house? Because a house that I won't be living in while I'm away halfway around the world trying to pay for it is no good for me. You might say that eventually, when I retire and move back to the Philippines, I'll still need a house. I can't argue with that. But one of the units in my building can serve as a primary residence when the time comes. And the good thing is, my building will keep on earning me money every month, but a house as my primary residence won't be able to do that. Unless of course I'm willing to share my house with strangers (i.e., rent out a room or two).

Another good thing about my building is that I paid it off in four years (i.e., the term of my personal loan in the UAE was only four years). Had I chosen to take out a mortgage in the Philippines for a house I wouldn't be able to enjoy as long as I'm an expat, it would have taken 30 years – the common mortgage tenure anywhere in the world – to pay off, not to mention the taxes, insurance and costs to maintain the property.

Does this mean I won't get any mortgage at all? No. I'm not one to swear off a mortgage. I know in the future, we might need to have one. And it's not considered a stupid debt if we are ready for it. Big ticket items like a house or a car really require intervention from financial institutions. But right now, I'm a happy renter.

I've been reading a lot on the requirements of home ownership though. This way, I won't be surprised when the right time to get a mortgage comes (if that time comes).

How to prepare for big-ticket item purchases like a house or a car

1. Avoid balloon loans as much as possible.

In a balloon loan or payment scheme, you take a mortgage or car financing that allows you to pay smaller amounts in the earlier terms of your loan and pay off a bigger lump sum at the end of the loan. This is very attractive for people who would want to purchase a house or a car (or both), but have limited repayment capacity at the moment, with the hopes of increasing their earning capacity later, well before the bigger lump sum payment comes.

(This is also applicable when taking a loan to put up a business. While the business hasn't taken off yet early into its opening, the business owner can pay off their business loan in smaller amounts, and ideally be able to pay the bigger lump sum at the end of the loan term, when the business is also earning more.)

The danger of balloon payments is that when the end of the loan comes and you don't have the capacity to pay for the lump sum, you might lose your house. Unlike a traditional mortgage, which is commonly 30 years long, a balloon mortgage would be a lot shorter, say five to seven years. In some cases, ten years is already long. And this is what makes it more challenging. You better be ready with the rest of the lender's money in that short amount of time.

Still, a lot of people take their chances with balloon mortgages. If by the end of the mortgage, they can't pay the lump sum, they either sell the property or take a personal loan to pay it off.

2. Save up for that customary 20% down payment.

If you don't have enough money for the down payment, there are two ways around this. First, you can try asking your financing institution if you could go for a lower percentage of down payment. In housing, this could go as low as 5% while when buying a car, a zero down payment is not uncommon.

However, I would certainly advise you against this first method, both for your house and your car, or for any other big purchases for that matter (e.g., business). This is mainly because when you borrow money for something, you would want enough down payment to ensure you have enough "ownership" of it such that whatever happens – perhaps you suddenly need to foreclose the property or give up your car for one reason or another – you wouldn't end up with nothing (or negative) after reselling. This is called having enough equity such that after selling an asset (e.g., worth AED 925,000 or ~USD 250,000) while still owing the bank money (e.g., worth AED 185,000 or ~USD 50,000), you'd still have profited (e.g., worth AED 740,000 or ~USD 200,000).

Moreover, having less than 20% down payment for a property gets pricier for you. More often than not, you're required to add and pay for a private mortgage insurance, to the tune of 0.5–2% of your loan's outstanding balance. Just as I mentioned earlier regarding insurance for personal loans, a private mortgage insurance is the same in that it is *not* for you. It's for the protection of your lender should you fail to make payments. Your insurance payments cease the moment you reach 20% equity in your property.

All in all, unless you can find a lender who won't mind not adding insurance payments onto your mortgage, the first workaround to buying a property or a car with less than a 20% down payment is not a good idea. Which brings us to the second and my highly recommended workaround: create a sinking fund for that 20% down payment (more on this in a later chapter).

I first read Robert Kiyosaki's book *Rich Dad, Poor Dad* when I was 19. At that time, I thought he was too brazen to make such a pragmatic statement that, contrary to popular belief, the house you bought with a mortgage is more of a liability than an asset.

Kiyosaki even listed all the reasons why it is a liability, but to sum it up, basically owning a house bleeds money, as is exhibited by all the extra expenses like property taxes, insurance and maintenance costs on top of the mortgage instalments you have to pay monthly.

As I've gotten older and learned more about the pros and cons of home ownership compared to renting, I can't help but agree with Kiyosaki's statement. However, I don't completely consider home ownership a terrible idea. It's always relative to your capacity and need.

In some situations, owning your own home is the better choice, despite it being more financially demanding compared to renting. If you are not put off by the idea of all the extras (e.g., property tax, insurance, maintenance costs) and if you are prepared for all of them, then you truly are a worthy homeowner.

With renting, the most that you will pay for is the rent itself (and the renter's insurance if you own valuable items inside your house that you want insured in case of theft or natural calamity). And that is its advantage over buying.

Be mindful though because the advantage of renting over buying is only fruitful if you invest your surplus (i.e., the money you were supposed to earmark for property tax, home ownership insurance, maintenance cost had you bought a property instead of rented). If you are renting and recklessly spending the rest of your money, then in your case, renting will never have an edge over owning the property itself. And don't get me started with the long-standing debate of renting vs. buying wherein renting is deemed as throwing away money while buying is an investment. It really is different from person to person and household to household.

SECTION TWO
MINDSET FIRST AND THE NUMBERS WILL FOLLOW

Of course, this book wouldn't be complete without talking about ways to get out of debt, or the more ideal scenario of preventing being in debt in the first place.

There is no secret as to how I have fully eradicated my consumer debts. In an earlier chapter, I mentioned my move to the UAE as an expatriate doing what I had already been doing in the Philippines. The only difference was the pay.

With my then new work in Abu Dhabi, I was able to earn 500% more than I used to get back in the Philippines. It was like receiving a *windfall* (e.g., an inheritance you weren't expecting, a huge dividend pay-out from an investment you had completely forgotten about).

Upon locking that new salary in, I realised that if you treat your new higher salary as a "monthly" windfall, there really are just two options: either you inflate your lifestyle and adjust your spending according to your new salary, or you manage your past money habits, settle all debt and start with a clean slate. Of course I chose the second option – otherwise I wouldn't be writing this book!

How did I do that? How was I able to resist the urge of a 500% increase in salary to buy all the luxury items and experiences that Dubai can offer?

Wiping my debt in the Philippines gave me an exhilarating feeling. It felt empowering! And instead of repeating the same mistakes and harbouring unnecessary debts again, I decided to change my money mindset by:

- channelling all my purchases to the things I really love. Let's call them *non-negotiables in life* as others have called them as well;
- seeing material things for what they truly are. I employ a *utilitarian* premise when buying stuff that I need;
- being grateful for every circumstance and person that gave me a leg-up in my debt-free journey. Recognising my *privileges* afforded me the idea that I can really and actually get out of the cycle of debt.

Allow me to tell you more about each of the above three strategies in the following chapters, and see Figure 2 below, with the changing mindset phase in bold.

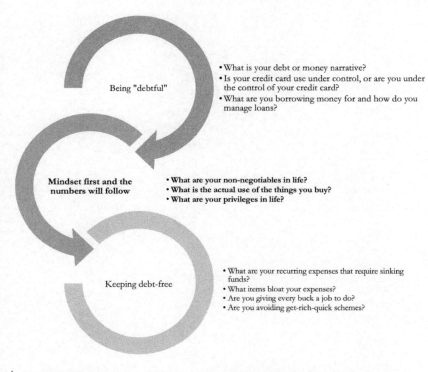

Figure 2. An overview of the reflective approach that guided my debt-free journey, with the focus on mindset

CHAPTER 4
IDENTIFYING MY NON-NEGOTIABLES IN LIFE

While writing this part, I was debating whether to put it in Chapter 6 when I discuss "privileges", or give it a chapter of its own. Ever since I decided to spend on things I truly needed and wanted, I became unapologetic with every purchase I made for myself. There is a certain sense of power from knowing what you truly desire in life, be it with your material needs and wants, experiences, or your entire why. It removes the shame and guilt in every purchase. That, for me, is a great privilege.

Because I know myself and I know what I truly desire in life, it makes every purchase mindful and meaningful. It also removes the feeling of fear of missing out (FOMO). There is no pressure to keep up and acquire the latest trends in areas that I do not truly care about. Ultimately, in trying to know yourself and what you truly desire, the best trick is to keep in mind what Oscar Wilde said: *"Be yourself; everyone else is already taken."*

What would happen if you didn't suffer from FOMO?

If friend #1 loves to collect watches, friend #2 likes shoes, and friend #3 is a bicycle addict, there's a tendency to keep up with all of them so as not to feel left out. You end up buying all that stuff plus all the other things you actually give a damn about. News flash (this shouldn't be a newsworthy kind of concept, but here it goes anyway): when your friends consume a lot of things they like, you don't have to have all of them as well, especially if your interest lies somewhere else. If you do that, and it's just simple maths, you end up with *less* money to buy what *you* actually like.

Why buy the same watches as friend #1 has, shoes as friend #2, and bikes as friend #3, when what you actually like are wigs (okay, that's a weird example, but go ahead and insert whatever you like in place of the word wigs). It could be plants or concert tickets. Can you imagine how many *more* plants you can purchase or concerts you can go to if you eliminate your spending on things that don't really matter to you? FOMO begets the need to keep up with the Joneses. No FOMO, no need to keep up! And you can focus on what you truly desire, without being influenced by prying eyes.

Reflect on the following questions:

- If all the material possessions in the world could only be seen by the owner and were invisible to the eyes of other people, what would be the things that you own? What would be the things that you will collect?
- If no other people can see your house except you, how big is your house going to be? Where are you going to be living?
- If you are only visible during your working hours and you become invisible after clocking out of work, what leisure activities would you be doing after work on your own or with people that truly matter?

If you think about it, the concepts above are all simply about not giving a damn. Now, I know these questions are in the superlative degree of being as hypothetical as they can get. But suppose we reflect on a more realistic scenario that is aligned to the hypothetical questions above.

"Imagine how we would be if we were less afraid."[1]

Imagine if you were less afraid about what people would say about the things you own, how will that affect the clothes you buy, your shoes, your bag, your car, your watch?

Imagine you were less afraid of what people would think about your home. How will that affect the size of your house or the neighbourhood you live in? Will you still aspire for that five-bedroom villa that is way out of your budget? Will you still want that four-bedroom townhouse in a highly affluent neighbourhood? Will you still wish to own that three-bedroom house in the suburbs when it is just you and your wife who are going to live in it? Barring valid questions like, *"But where will my guests sleep when they are visiting?"* if you are less afraid about what other people would say about where you live and how big your house is, always go for what you can afford to pay first and foremost, according to the size of your family, in a safe neighbourhood.

Remember, *you* are the one who's going to sign up for that mortgage (if you are buying) or that lease (if you are renting), *you* are the one who will pay for it monthly, not other people, not the ones who are passing by in front of your house, and certainly not the ones you are trying to impress. Paying a way higher amount of rent than you can afford each month could really eat into your income.

Having a mortgage is not a joke either. It's insane to have one just to put up an image of being a rich homeowner. If you miscalculate what you truly need for a house versus what you think you should have because others might judge how tiny your house is or how "poor" your neighbourhood is, it is highly likely you'll end up paying for that house until you die. The etymological meaning of mortgage is "dead pledge", coming from the Latin word *"mortuus"* meaning dead, and French word *"gage"* meaning pledge. If that word doesn't seem like it's enough warning on its own against overspending on your house, I don't know any other word that will!

As for the question of where your guests will be staying, keep in mind that your guests will be visiting you, not your house. Be creative! Moreover, whoever is capable of travelling a distance to see you surely has the means to stay in a hotel in your area.

Imagine if you were less afraid of being yourself in front of your friends and colleagues, how would that affect your hobbies and recreational activities? Every now and then, a trendy activity comes along, and through bandwagon appeal, most people would want to try it. Which begs the question, *"Are they doing that activity because they really want to try it?"* or *"Are they doing that because they don't want to be left behind by their friends who have already tried it?"*

See, with the former, you have someone who has a genuine interest to try that activity. But with the latter, you have someone who is protecting their image. They are afraid they would be branded as lame for not having tried the current craze in town. It takes away from their cool points.

That mindset is not limited to trendy activities alone. This could also apply to perpetually harmful habits that require no trendsetting techniques or appeals for people to buy into. Do you have vices that you cannot seem to shake off even if you know they are not good for you? I have heard a lot about chronic smokers or drinkers whom when you ask about when and how they began the habit, almost always answered something like, *"I tried it with a friend when I was younger, and I haven't been able to stop ever since."* Or, *"I started as an occasional smoker/drinker because it looks really cool, plus all my officemates do it during our breaks, so…"*

Choose one thing that you are ultimately passionate about and have no shame about buying it so no matter what you choose to spend your money on, you know you like it, you need it for yourself, and you truly desire it. It was not a purchase borne out of your need to impress other people, which is a catalyst for unwanted consumer debts. And if you can afford it, it doesn't even have to be just one thing.

Over the past few years, I have learned what I truly like in life. My craving for these things and experiences could change in the foreseeable future, but right now, I feel fortunate to know what things I consider significant in my life. Knowing this means I get to buy them, own them, and spend my money on them mindfully and unapologetically. Financially mindful people call them *non-negotiables in life* because by hook or by crook, they should have a place in their budget, or else, they would probably end up feeling like they are working and working for money they don't even get to enjoy, which is a no-no for them. It should be for us as well! My non-negotiables in life have changed over the years as newer interests have slowly crept in and older ones slipped out.

Right now, my non-negotiables in life are books, travel, and board games. It used to include concert tickets. I loved seeing various alternative rock bands perform live. There was also baking, and I would try to buy all the nice equipment related to baking. Then there was scuba diving. The equipment for scuba diving isn't cheap at all. Ideally, any diver can rent what is needed, but since I knew I'd be doing it for the long haul, I decided to have my own. Diving trips cost a lot too, what with all the boats and its crew to assist you. But it somehow was aligned with my other non-negotiable in life – travel – so I didn't mind the costs of all my diving trips, one of which was diving in the Great Barrier Reef. I had only seen the Great Barrier Reef on the Discovery Channel or the National Geographic Channel when I was younger. I knew I wanted to see it one day with my own eyes. Since it was one of my ultimate desires at that time, I made sure to grab that experience without any hesitation as to the possible cost. When you know yourself and you know what you truly desire, you are prepared to pay for that non-negotiable no matter what.

MY NON-NEGOTIABLE IN LIFE #1

Books! These have been one of my very first purchases since I started earning a living as a young professional. Upon receiving my first salary as a clinical practitioner, I went straight to the National Bookstore branch nearest my workplace and bought two novels and three autobiographies.

Prior to that, I'd never owned any books for leisure reading, and only read what I could borrow from my school and university libraries. When I was younger, it was never a priority in our household to read for pleasure or do anything that would cost my parents a single peso which they thought was better off spent on basic needs. So, unlike children who grew up burying their noses in books their parents bought for them, I unfortunately had very little opportunity to read for pleasure while growing up.

The want to read has always been there, but I knew better than to ask my parents for money to buy books. Hence, for entertainment, we relied solely on any activities that were free, such as playing tag outside the house, climbing trees, flying kites made of recycled materials, and more.

All in all, it wasn't that bad, and the only limitation was our imagination. Still, I've always wondered how I would have turned out if I'd started reading as a habit early on. I'm only wondering because at my current rate of book consumption, I have already made great strides in my personal development, emotionally (e.g., empathy), cognitively (e.g., critical thinking), and socially (e.g., stronger sense of community), that I would have never previously thought possible just by immersing myself in the habit of reading.

I consider books as an investment to my knowledge, which is why I always pay for them. I'm quite familiar with the habit of a lot of people who "pirate" books and never pay a single dime for any book they can get their hands on for free via the internet.

Yes, there is a certain sense of pride that comes when you obtain something for free while others paid for it with their hard-earned money. It would seem as if you are wiser than the rest for acquiring the same thing for free. But just like any other service, authors provide us with the service to inform (especially for non-fiction) and the service to entertain. The amount of time, expertise and creative prowess required to come up with a book is no easy feat (I should know, I'm writing one right now!), hence, I strongly believe that no one is in a position to obtain any book through piracy and think they deserve to own that book for free. Of course, you can still get a lot of free books nowadays, either as a gift from someone else or as a promotional strategy of the author.

Speaking of gifts, books are also my favourite kind of gift to give, especially to kids. Perhaps, it is a habit borne out of the fact that I never owned any books as a child. Or perhaps it is the joy I feel whenever I get to kindle a reading habit within another human being.

I can't imagine not reading a part of a book every single day. I believe, among my non-negotiables, this one will stay forever. At one point, I even dreamt of having my own library in my own home (not anymore though). But despite losing that dream to the convenience of owning everything digitally, my love and need for books hasn't waned even for a little bit. In fact, my appetite for reading keeps on growing by the day.

As of writing, I read and collect my books through my Kindle account. I still have my very first Kindle – a third generation one with the cute keyboard – but I currently read using my iPad. I realised that having an electronic version of the books I wanted to read was much more manageable in terms of space than if I were to buy all of them and stack them at home.

I have moved eleven times across three countries in the past 25 years. The earlier moves – these happened when I was a student up to my young professional years – were quite hard because of the massive amounts of books I had, both for academia and for leisure reading. When I moved from the Philippines to the UAE, it stung a bit to leave all my books behind. And that is when I came up with my resolve to, except for gifted books, only keep electronic versions of my books. And that made all the recent moves much easier.

MY NON-NEGOTIABLE IN LIFE #2

Travel! I try to travel to a new-to-me place at least once each year. This is non-negotiable. For me, travelling is both a pleasure and a challenge rolled into one. It is a respite I give to my tired self, away from the usual day-to-day hustle of life. It is also a lesson I give to myself as I try and expand my horizons.

When travelling, despite careful planning, I don't know what is going to happen next until the moment is already happening. It gives me something to look forward to and something to be prepared for. Travelling tests my character: my patience, my tolerance, my aptitude, my sense of security. Travelling also busts the myths and stereotypes I have in mind as I try and navigate the various cultural tapestries I face during my travels, near and far. Whether short or long, my travels contribute to deepening my cultural sensitivity.

These are only some of the benefits I get from travelling, but they are the most important ones for me. I could not think of any other activity in the world that would give me all these benefits in one go. Patience, tolerance, and cultural sensitivity are built over time, not achieved over night. That is all the more reason to travel often and to start as soon as possible.

Although my primary reasons for travelling are quite philosophical in nature, I still relish the usual joys one gets from travelling, such as trying out the local cuisine, seeing the scenery, watching a local show, and simply being there. These experiences are actually what would supply the aforementioned character-building opportunities I get from travelling.

What is the custom when eating this local dish or at that restaurant? How do I use public transport to get to that place? How should I behave amidst a sea of locals and tourists also watching this concert/musical/show? How does me being here, being able to rest, being open to these new experiences make me feel? I would pay the premium – plane tickets, hotel bookings, pocket money – to be able to answer all these questions at least once a year.

In another strategy I mention in a later chapter, I will share with you how I save for my trips to make sure I have the funds to do this non-negotiable thing in my life and not go into debt.

You can define your non-negotiables more specifically if you want to. With travel, I already mentioned that at least one new place a year is enough. For the mechanics of travel, I like flying comfortably so I need to make sure I have sufficient money to buy a seat where I will feel comfortable for the entire duration of a flight.

I feel so cramped with most airlines' legroom in economy. I'm not saying that because I'm a fussy person, but because I'm 5 feet 7 inches tall, and most of my height comes from my long thighs and legs, not my spine. If you are thinking I always fly business, then you are thinking wrong. I have flown a few business flights, yes. But they were all free upgrades. Yes! I'm so lucky like that.

Right now, I prefer to fly premium economy for longer than six hours of flight and economy with extra legroom seats for any flight less than six hours. I'm a sucker for exit row seats! If the day comes when I can part with my money to buy business class seats without feeling guilty about their cost or the dent it would make in my savings, then I would gladly enjoy myself up there.

For now, I'm happy to be in coach and pay extra to grab the exit row seats or extra legroom seats. I'm not ashamed to admit that because travelling is not even a basic need, being able to travel is already a luxury for me and for most.

For accommodation, I'm in the middle of the spectrum. I do not go for the cheapest accommodation, nor do I go for the most expensive. Apart from hotels, I have tried staying in entire flats and houses listed on Airbnb. Anything goes. But I'm not a fan of the concept *"okay na yang mura, tutulugan lang naman"* (the cheap ones will do, you will just sleep on it anyway). What if they are cheap because they are not well-maintained?

Dingy accommodation is already out. Privacy is of utmost importance, so hostels are also out. For month-long trips, I need a washing machine inside my accommodation so I can wash my clothes as needed. I'm not very rigid on needing in-hotel breakfasts because looking for a breakfast nook around the area is one part of our travel itinerary that I enjoy doing.

For trips that would entail me to stay in one place and not have to walk around town, a nice all-inclusive resort hotel is more than welcome. All in all, I always search for new hotels (guaranteed cleaner than most) that are within the city centre (makes it easier to go around). If nothing is available in the city centre by the time of booking, anywhere outside but with a nearby metro station will do. Clean and easily accessible. That sums up my accommodation requirements.

MY NON-NEGOTIABLE IN LIFE #3

Board games! This might be counter-intuitive with my decision to collect electronic versions of my books instead of print, because board game boxes are even bigger than books. But, yes, board games are one of my non-negotiables in life.

I like them and the hobby for a lot of reasons, with my top two being: (1) it allows me to challenge myself cognitively (especially through playing games with higher complexity) and (2) it allows me to escape from all the modern-day technological pitfalls (i.e., doom-scrolling, binge-watching) with ease. Meeting and playing with new people who are into the hobby of tabletop gaming also gives me an avenue for community integration and socialisation. And just like travelling, I'm willing to pay a premium – buying and collecting board games, having enough space at home to collect them, and being ready to pay for a safer way to transport my entire collection should I need to move – to enjoy the benefits of board gaming.

Board game collecting is one of those things that could easily get out of hand if you aren't careful about what you really want to own. Without careful planning, without setting ground rules as to what should be added into your own collection, and without quenching the fire of envy and the need to keep the image of "having it all", you might end up with a watered-down collection with half of the items not even to your liking, taking up so much of your precious space at home and separating you from your hard-earned money.

How do we avoid physical collections from getting out of hand?

Reflect on the following items to try to know yourself better and what you truly desire in material things and experiences.

- Think of a set of things/experiences that you collect.
- Why do you collect them?
- Did you see someone else's collection before you started your own?
- Are any of your friends collecting them as well?
- Who started collecting first, you or your friend/s?
- Do you feel any pressure whenever your friend/s add something to their own collection while you do not have that same item/experience yet?
- Do you collect at your own pace, or do you feel the need to always have the most complete collection against other people you know are collecting the same items/experiences too?

When I started my board game collection in 2014, I told myself I would only buy one game per month. Because there were simply too many options out there in the market, there were months when I didn't buy anything because I got overwhelmed by the possibilities of owning this worker placement game or that deck-building one.

As a matter of fact, I had a very tiny collection of a measly ten games between 2014 and 2018. My friends and I were just enjoying and optimising the use of all my games and I would only buy a new board game when I felt like I wanted a "palate cleanser" away from my old ones.

I was happy with the steady state rise of my board game collection because every purchase felt like a natural progression from my old game to the next new one, both in terms of theme and complexity. Everything worked out fine until 2019 when a colleague-turned-friend of mine asked if she could explore my collection and try out playing some games with us. She was introduced to board gaming by one of her couple friends and immediately got hooked.

We began playing more frequently each week. While she was building her own collection, my rate of acquiring of board games picked up exponentially compared to the previous years when I was happy rotating my less than ten board games. But it picked up only to the rate that I originally planned: one new board game per month (I assure you this is nothing compared to other board game enthusiasts out there).

I felt I had to keep acquiring new ones so we could try out more varied games since it was quite rare to meet someone who had the same level of interest in playing board games as I do. I was not keeping up with her collection, I was keeping up with the energy of us yearning to try out something new each chance we got.

Despite increasing my rate of purchasing new board games, I never got into any debt whatsoever. I did, however, purchase more than one game per month during sale seasons. Nevertheless, every purchase was well thought out. I created a separate spreadsheet to list all the games I might like, alongside columns of criteria like complexity, average rating by other board gamers, designer (there are specific board game designers whose games I adore), publisher (there are specific publishers known for producing excellent game components), and price.

If a certain game I was eyeing up didn't meet my threshold for each criterion, then it would be moved to another tab labelled "Changed my mind". In short, I do not just purchase any game I see. I didn't impulse buy any of the board games in my collection. I'm quite sure that among my network of board gamers, I have the smallest collection. But it does not deter me from enjoying the hobby.

Nowadays, I'm still debt-free because of my non-negotiables. I owe a lot to my non-negotiables because my money doesn't go anywhere that's not important for me. No matter what trend passes by, I'm secure *not* to ride on it if it's not part of what I prioritise in life. I'm resilient to fads and the bandwagon appeal because I can rely on my list of priorities and non-negotiables to serve as my North Star as to where my money should go.

CHAPTER 5
USING THE UTILITARIAN PREMISE

I n this day and age of excessive consumerism, buying luxury items for ordinary everyday things like clothes and shoes is not unheard of. Gone are the days when you only see designer bags and clothes on celebrities and the elite. Anyone who can borrow money – more specifically anyone who has a credit card – can buy whatever they want, so much so that it has become a *race*. The first ones to get the latest iPhone, the latest pieces of Balenciaga, and the limited-edition watch collaboration by Swatch and Omega are deemed "way cooler" than the rest of us.

There are those who buy these things because they need and can truly afford them. And there are those who have an ulterior motive for owning such trendy items. It's never a crime to buy something just to be on trend, to flaunt, or to show people that you can. But I hope you'll be sensible enough to draw the line if you're buying them, going into debt, and losing your peace of mind thinking about how to repay that debt, all for the reason of wanting to look cool.

If the motive behind buying these luxury items is to flaunt them and try to draw people's attention to your "rich-looking lifestyle", I guarantee you that they can't see it. Why? Because they're also too busy flaunting what they bought, they really don't have time to look at other people's stuff (and possibly thinking about their debts too).

Do you know what the truly wealthy people actually buy? Or how much they spend on average on everyday things like clothes, shoes, watch, or their car? I recommend you read *The Millionaire Next Door* by Thomas J. Stanley and William D. Danko.

This sort of spending isn't only about buying luxury items out of someone's price range, it's also about buying dozens of ordinary items they already have. How many white sneakers does one person really need at a time? How many black leather belts does one need to own? And when malls and shops go on sale, do you really have to buy something if you don't need it?

What was my antidote to all the excessive consumption that mired me in tens of thousands of consumer debt under my name in the past? Simple. I tried to view each item using a utilitarian lens: buy each item according to its usefulness.

For the rest of this chapter, I'll be sharing how I applied the utilitarian concept to reflect and justify most of my purchases. I wrote them as a checklist that won't take a minute to go through. I hope it helps you in mindfully buying your next mobile phone, watch, clothes, shoes, bags, make-up and perfume, cars, and even plan that next trip.

NB: I'm using the word *utility* here because I want to emphasise purchasing based primarily on the basic *use* of objects and any of our material possessions. So, when I say utilitarian, I'm not referring to the ethical theory of *utilitarianism* that proposes that a chosen action is considered right as long as it promotes happiness and contributes to the happiness of the greater good. Although, if we're trying to eliminate money anxiety and raise happiness in the process of being debt-free, we might as well be talking about utilitarianism too, in its essence.

MOBILE PHONES

Do you know someone who always has the latest iPhone and who always gets it within days of its release? I'm not just talking about anyone who has the latest iPhone. A lot of iPhone users can afford to pay for it without going into debt, even if they keep on updating their phone every year.

I'm talking about someone who is still paying instalments for their iPhone from last year and are already lining up to take the latest iPhone. I have always wondered how they keep up with their payments if they keep on upgrading to the latest one and going into debt in the process. I guess being trendy and "in" is really a great motivator to subject oneself to an awful lot of debt.

Good thing Apple has that trade-in scheme wherein you can have your iPhone (and other Apple products) assessed for credit so whatever you buy next will cost less than its actual price. But it still begs the question of whether it really is worth it to go into debt just to have the latest phone when your current one is working fine. Again, view it as a tool, in a utilitarian perspective.

The following checklist, and the succeeding ones in this chapter, look like they are written for a kindergartner. Do not worry, they have been deliberately written that way to keep everything straightforward. They're so simple, it's like *duh*! But we get into debt because we're afraid to confront such basic questions.

Remember, more often than not, the reason why we are submerged in a crippling amount of debt is because of our past stupid money decisions. So, do not underestimate the power of a simple checklist to keep you from repeating your old mistakes.

Check this one out about whether you need to borrow money to buy the latest phone or not.

"Do I need to go into debt to get the latest [insert phone model here]?" checklist

---

- Can my phone still make and receive calls?
- Can my phone still send and receive messages?
- Are the cameras still able to **take photos/videos** and whatnots?
- Does my phone still **run well** with all my *needed* apps installed on it? (I emphasised the needed apps because a phone will definitely lag if you install a whole lot of unnecessary apps.)
- Are all the other uses of my phone still working?
- Do I still have consumer debts right now? Am I bothered that I'm not making progress in lowering them?

If you answered yes to all the questions above, perhaps it is not a good idea to buy/swap your current phone if it will set you back a couple of hundred or thousand bucks while still in consumer debt.

WATCH

Times have changed (pun intended) and with it, the utility of watches. Nowadays, watches are not just used to tell time. Our phones can even do that. Had the world not made watches to be so smart, they would have become obsolete by now.

Today, instead of having a single watch to tell the time, we have an array of watches. Each one does something very specific (e.g., dive computer, altimeter watch, fitness band, etc.) or does everything all at once, i.e., a smartwatch.

While owning one of each type of watch is completely justified for their specialised feature and accuracy regarding their related activity, owning dozens of *everyday watches* with different colours and styles is something that needs rationalisation, if using the utilitarian lens.

In the world of fashion, it makes sense to have different coloured watches and different styles to match your top or your bottom or your shoes or your hair or the occasion. Under the utilitarian premise though, we go after the use of that watch.

I own *one* "everyday watch", which was a gift from my partner. Apart from it, I own *one* specialised watch for each activity I do: one for diving and one smartwatch for my workouts. On top of these three watches, I do not really feel the need to have more.

Maybe in the future, when I start to feel the need to climb Mt. Everest or Mont Blanc, I would definitely buy myself an altimeter watch. Perhaps, I need to own one dress watch, but I do not really attend any events that require me to wear one.

"Do I really need that expensive watch?" checklist

- Do I have an "everyday" watch that I can use right now?
- Does my current "everyday" watch still **tell time**? (For an everyday watch, I think there is no other utilitarian reason for its existence other than to tell time.)
- Do I still have consumer debts right now? Am I bothered by their presence?

If you answered yes to all the questions above, then, from a utilitarian perspective, you truly do not need that expensive watch right now.

"Do I really need a new fitness/diving/smart/altimeter/other watch?" checklist

---

- Do I already own a fitness/diving/smart/altimeter/other that I can use right now or is there someone I can borrow this from for the time being?
- Do I still have consumer debts right now? Am I bothered by their presence?

If you answered yes to both questions, then you do not need that new watch.

CLOTHES

What is the purpose of clothes? In a civilised society, clothes are compulsory as they keep our bodies covered, allowing us to maintain our modesty and dignity. Moreover, depending on the environment, clothes also allow our bodies to keep warm or cool. Specialised clothes also protect us from hazardous events or materials.

Throughout the centuries, clothes have also signified status and identity, which, even nowadays are reflected through the works of the fashion industry. I'm not a fashion expert, but a quick search will tell you that the fashion industry is categorised into three main types:

- *haute couture* (e.g., custom-made Dior, Chanel, Balenciaga, Valentino, etc.);
- *ready-to-wear* (e.g., off-the-rack Dior, Chanel, Balenciaga, Valentino, etc.); and
- *mass market* (e.g., Gap, Zara, H&M, etc.).

From the few examples above, you can tell I refer to the mass market brands as the *ordinary* brands, and the ready-to-wear and haute couture as the *luxury* brands. It's quite obvious that even the ready-to-wear ones are not readily accessible to the masses, despite its name. So, for the rest of this chapter, I will simplify our brand categories and label them *ordinary* or *luxury.*

But why do people go into debt to buy luxury pieces of clothing despite it being out of their price range? The simple answer is, they really do look good and feel good on your body.

But is it really sufficiently good to be in debt for? Or do we buy these things because we see our celebrity idols wearing them? In a design and style masterclass delivered by *Queer Eye* co-host Tan France, he said that although it is nice to own the designer pieces we usually see on celebrities, he was kind enough to remind viewers that most of these pieces are given or lent to them by the design house.

In most situations, they do not have to pay hundreds or thousands of dollars to wear these luxury pieces in public, by way of sponsorship. And while most of us would want to look like our celebrity idols, Tan France reiterated that we need to be careful in chasing the thrill of owning what celebrities wear, as purchasing those items could really be costly for the general public.

It was refreshing to hear someone in the fashion industry say this, because not a lot of people, especially those with such power to influence, would be this candid about being practical and responsible when purchasing and owning high fashion items.

"Do I really need that designer dress/top?" checklist

- If I buy from a non-designer label, would it be able to **cover my body and keep me modest** in the same way a designer brand would?
- Do I still have something in my timeless pieces of clothes that I can wear for this particular event?
- Are my clothes still visually appealing (i.e., no discolouration, no fraying, etc.)?
- Am I only eyeing up that designer dress/top so people would think I'm rich?
- Do I still have consumer debts right now? Am I bothered by their presence?

If you answered yes to all the questions above, then buying an expensive clothing article right now might not do your budget and current debt any good.

I personally love clothing brands Uniqlo and Muji. Almost all the basics I bought from these shops have stood the test of time. I had a season in my life when I started to covet designer clothing pieces. I tried buying a piece or two every now and then, and to my surprise, it really didn't improve my utility of clothes in any way. Yes, there is a difference in the look and feel of the material when compared to my usual clothes, but other than that, I was still as covered and as modest as I was when wearing my mass market produced clothes. I was not any happier or more satisfied in life wearing those designer items compared to when I was wearing my usual clothes. That goes for designer shoes too.

SHOES

Just like that season in my life when I started trying out designer clothes, my season of owning designer shoes didn't last. I bought a few pairs, and I gave them all away after a few uses.

I have had better pairs that didn't even cost me a lot – and I used to own *a lot* of pairs of shoes in my 20s and early 30s, so my frame of reference is quite wide. And do not get me started on how uncomfortable and impractical those designer shoes were, especially when worn for more than four hours.

Right now, I don't own a lot of shoes. As with my watch, I just have sufficient pairs to address each area of my life.

I have at most, at any given point, two pairs of casual shoes for going out, which I replace as soon as the heels and arches start feeling uncomfortable.

For cycling, I own a pair of shoes for road biking and a separate one for mountain biking.

For overseas travel, I keep one pair of shoes designed for long trekking, and another one for hiking in a sub-zero environment.

For a more formal look, I own two pairs of dress boots (one knee-high, one ankle-high).

For physical activities, I have one pair of shoes for outdoor running and another pair for indoor training, both of which I replace religiously when they reach their maximum mileage. Current guidelines suggest that we replace our running shoes after 500–800 kilometres of usage or every six months, whichever comes first.

Since I'm on sabbatical at the time of writing, I do not currently own any office shoes. When I do get employed again, I will add them to my shoe needs.

I used to have a pair of shoes for triathlon, but I have not trained for it in years. If I do decide to pick up that sport again, I will add another pair of shoes to my currently owned ones.

So, all in all, that is a total of ten pairs of shoes. According to a poll conducted in the US, most women own, on average, 19 pairs of shoes – almost 200% of what I currently own – with only four pairs being worn regularly.[1] In the UK, the average is 34 pairs of shoes![2]

"Do I need that pair of designer shoes?" checklist

- Do I currently have a pair of shoes and a spare for my everyday work?
- Are my walking/running/gym/sports shoes still within their appropriate mileage?
- If I attend that party, will my old pair of dress shoes go well with the dress/suit I'm going to wear?
- Do I still have consumer debts right now? Am I bothered by their presence?

If you answered yes to all the questions above, then you probably do not need that extra pair of shoes.

BAGS

Have you noticed that bags nowadays are being used as an accessory as much as for their original use: to hold and keep your personal items together while you move around? Sometimes, even more so as an accessory. And how many bags does a person need to own? Just like shoes, I guess it is safe to say one bag for each field of use is enough.

There's no point in having more than one because, for example, if you play tennis, you can just carry the one tennis bag that has your first-choice racket, and enough space for a couple more alternative rackets, just in case. You would definitely look stupid if you came to a tennis court carrying five different tennis bags when all your rackets could have easily been carried in one bag.

It's also quite unheard of that you carry five Louis Vuitton handbags to the office on any given day, so why is there a need to own and keep all five or more when you can only utilise one at a time? It probably is not about utility anymore. It is about looking good, making sure your bag goes with your dress or suit.

It might also be because it makes one look rich; the constant swapping of bags each day surely makes you look like you have a lot of disposable income to buy and own all of them. Now, there is *nothing* inherently wrong with owning a lot of bags for any of the reasons above, especially for those who can afford them and not be driven into debt to achieve a certain look with the bags they are flaunting around. But, for the nth time, if you are a person with debt as tall as the Burj Khalifa and you are bothered by it, then is it really worth it to stack your debt even higher just for a bag?

"Do I need that luxury bag?" checklist

- If I buy a leather bag from a non-luxury label, will it be able to **hold and keep my things** as well as the one with a designer label?
- From the bags I currently own, do I have something that would go well with my outfit?
- Am I only eyeing up this bag because I want to flaunt it in the office on Monday?
- Am I only buying this bag so people will think I'm rich?

- Am I only buying this bag because it would be humiliating if I'm the only one *not* joining this trend? (Typical FOMO.)
- Do I still have consumer debts right now? Am I bothered by their presence?

If you answered yes to all the questions above, then you do not need that luxury bag right now.

MAKE-UP AND PERFUME

I have had my fair share of make-up and perfume from designer brands, and I must say, they really are good. Excellent coverage and not cakey for the foundations; good hold for the mascaras, tints and shadows; an awesome and long-lasting smell for the perfumes. But there are brands that deliver the same quality and won't break the bank.

I remember buying make-up from designer brands, but I didn't know how to apply make-up to save my life (this is still true today). And when I started looking at YouTube videos to learn the basic principles of make-up application, I saw that some make-up gurus were using brands that were not as high end as the ones I had bought, and yet their make-up application was still a thousand times better than mine.

I believe technique is a crucial factor in make-up application and no amount of expensive make-up brands could ever magically make my application any more fabulous. And no matter what I did, I couldn't finish the entire contents – be it a bottle of perfume, an eye shadow, a liquid foundation – before I bought another one!

Of course, I'm not like this anymore. But I remember it came to a point when it became so hard to justify buying one item after another without having finished the previous one yet.

Others like having bags and bags of make-up and bottle after bottle of perfume, perhaps a different scent for each day or mood. It simply doesn't make sense going into further debt to buy more of the things you already have and are still perfectly usable. But if you are not in crippling debt, have excellent savings and make-up and perfumes are part of your non-negotiables, then you're good.

"Do I need more make-up and perfume?" checklist

- If I buy make-up/perfume from a non-luxury/non-designer brand, will it be able to **make me as pretty and good smelling** as the one from a more expensive label?
- Do I still have a make-up set and perfume that I can use?
- Am I only buying these new sets of make-up and perfume because they are the latest trends right now?
- Do I still have consumer debts right now? Am I bothered by their presence?

If you answered yes to all the questions above, then you do not need that new bag of make-up or new bottle of perfume right now.

CARS

In an earlier chapter, I mentioned that I don't own a car right now. But if I were to get one, I would want to have a brand new one, or a used one in excellent condition. I also did say I like commuting via public transport, which begs the question as to why I would need to buy a car.

Simple: to get from point A to point B much faster, especially when I'm carrying a lot of things! I love using public transport, but it has its disadvantages as well, such as the multiple transfers (depending on the destination), the possible delays, the limited baggage you can bring with you, and the lack of personal space.

Moreover, depending on where my work is going to be and the

location of my house, I might actually need to drive to get around especially if moving immediately is not an option.

Just like our small everyday items (clothes, shoes, bags), some people are in way over their heads when it comes to their capacity to buy a car. They are after the cool points instead of its use.

But buying a car is already expensive in and of itself, therefore why not buy a cool one so it's worth your buck? That's a valid point. And I will repeat my answer from the earlier items: if the debt does not bother you, go ahead and buy that cool car you want! But if you're sacrificing your mental health for a few cool points, you might want to reconsider what car to purchase. Remember, you're the one who's going to be stuck with monthly payments, *not* the people around you whom you expect to say "ooooh" and "aaaaah" to your car.

"Do I need that brand new luxury car?" checklist

- Can my current car safely bring me from point A (current location) to point B (destination)?
- Are my family's transport needs still being covered by our current car/s?
- Am I only eyeing up this car because I want to have the coolest car among my colleagues and friends?
- Am I only buying this car so people will think I'm rich?
- Do I still have consumer debts right now? Am I bothered by their presence?

If you answered yes to all the questions above, trust me, you do not really need that brand new luxury car right now.

OVERSEAS TRIPS

If you ask anyone who takes international trips regularly as to why they do that, their answers are likely to be along the following lines:

- Because I need a break from work to recharge.
- Because my kids are on a school break, and I would like to take them on this trip so they can keep it as part of their core childhood memories.
- Because we need to spend time as a family away from the busyness of life.
- Because I want to see/walk/climb/be in [*insert something ancient or wonderful here*] in person.
- Because I love food and I want to taste the most authentic [*insert dish name or cuisine here*].

And while taking a trip can get very expensive especially for the whole family, it is all worth it if done for the right reasons, coupled with a healthy financial plan for it. If you are still taking vacations while in crippling debt simply because you want to have something to post on your social media for everyone to see, then you might need to re-evaluate your priorities in life. Because being in debt just to flaunt your trips has never done anyone's mental health any good.

If you couple practicality with delayed gratification, you might even find alternative activities you can do during your time off work in lieu of going on a trip. Just be sure to choose an activity that could also have the same effect as an overseas trip – mainly relaxation and recreation – without having to be as costly as flying out of the country.

"Do I need this vacation right now?" checklist

- Am I only taking this trip because others are taking trips as well and I do not want to look like I'm being left behind while everyone is out of the country?

- Am I only taking this trip so I have something new to post on my social media feed? (You might think this assumption is too shallow, but it happens around us *a lot* more often than we care to acknowledge.)
- Am I still behind with my debt repayments?
- Would I be willing to delay treating myself to a trip so I can redirect my money to pay down more debts or save up for this trip so I do not perpetuate being in a cycle of debt?

If you answered yes to all the questions above, trust me, you do not really need that trip right now.

After almost four decades of revolving around the sun, after massive shifts in my taste in clothes and other material things, I realised that owning fancy things can be a good experience, but the quest is quite unappealing in that once you get to own what you want, after a day or two, the *temporary high* passes and you find yourself already looking forward to buying the next big thing.

Unless you are a one-percenter, there will always be someone with a better suit, better pair of shoes, better jewellery, better car. So, chasing more expensive things that are out of your price range is not a good idea because there is going to be no end in sight. A lifestyle like this will give you a mindset that nothing is ever enough.

Trying out those designer items made me realise that they are not for me, even if I have the means to buy them. I don't want to sound like I have transcended having to own nice things. I'm far from that. But right now, I'm aware of the things I want to own, and I will stick with that awareness. I don't consider it as a lifestyle downgrade. It's simply streamlining my lifestyle.

CHAPTER 6
RECOGNISING MY PRIVILEGES

R ecognise your privileges and keep them in mind as you sort your debts out. Your privileges will be a constant reminder that you are not starting at the first step in this journey. You already have boosters!

We all know that, despite effortful and impactful social campaigns, current societal norms still see a certain race, or gender, or socioeconomic status as an advantage for employment, career advancement, and more. A person who has one, two, or all of these 'favourable' characteristics could be looked upon by others as privileged.

But these are not the privileges that I'll be referring to in this chapter because in my case, I'm certainly not advantaged in any of those areas, but I sure am 100% debt-free. And I'm grateful for a couple of privileges in my life that put me at an advantage of not having to owe the government, financing institutions, or anyone any money.

A FULLY PAID FOR DEGREE

I was able to obtain a university degree without having to borrow a single peso. Why is this so important? Because I didn't end up with a massive student loan. This doesn't mean that those with student loans are considered unprivileged. No. Not at all! It depends on how you look at the situation. Those with student loans got a complete higher education in exchange for that loan, right? A college degree is indeed a privilege, and if used wisely, it can be one of the greatest weapons against crippling debt. A student loan for education is similar to taking a business loan to put up a business. It's all part of the "capital" for your investment.

Who should I thank for this privilege? Of course, my parents who fully paid for my degree. Double thanks to them for having the sense to pre-pay my college degree by investing in an educational plan.

Thanks to the Philippine government as well for not making such a huge fuss about the student loan trend that has befallen the US and other countries. I hate a lot of things about the Philippine government and how they run the country, but I like the fact that they do not condemn us to take out such massive student loans early on in our lives. Come to think of it, there are a few questions that pop into my head whenever the subject of student loans is brought up:

- Why are there no student loan schemes available in the Philippines? Is it because we do not have enough lending power to allow people to take such loans?
- If there are student loan schemes in the Philippines, do you think more of us would take advantage of them and undertake higher education? Consequently, will this help to reduce the unemployment rate or the poverty level in our country? How will this affect our economy?
- If we did take advantage of the student loan scheme (if it existed in the Philippines), do you think we would be better off like our contemporaries in the US and other countries who also took student loans? Or would we also struggle paying the loan off just like them?

A smart way to avoid a massive student debt

Back when I was a college instructor of physiotherapy in the Philippines, I noticed that I started having a higher number of

Filipino-American students in my class. These Filipino-American students of mine were born and raised in the US. They studied in the US from grade school until they finished their senior year. They then flew and stayed in the Philippines to study physiotherapy.

Regardless of how they paid for their studies in the Philippines (i.e., most likely their parents in the US sent them the money), when they returned to the US, they went back with a full bachelor's degree and *zero* student loan.

They then took the exam that will qualify them to work as physiotherapists in the US and started working right away. With that strategy, they are way ahead of their contemporaries in the wealth-accumulation stage since they do not have a massive student loan to pay off. What a smart move!

THE ABILITY TO CHOOSE WORK

Most expats in the UAE are there for one reason: greener pastures. Whether we came to the UAE because we needed a new environment, we were running away from bad memories at home, or we were nursing a broken heart, we stayed for one good reason: a better income compared to what we would get back home. I'm sorry. Let me correct that: a *tax-free* income at a better rate compared to what we would get back home. There, I said it. I'm not even going to deny that that is one of the primary reasons I have stayed in the UAE for a decade.

I first started looking at employment prospects in the UAE when I visited my sister and her family in Dubai back in 2013. I was on a two-month summer break from my then work at a university in Manila. My sister and brother-in-law floated the idea of me moving to the UAE permanently.

So, while I was staying with them in Dubai during those two months, I didn't waste any time in between our excursions to look for jobs that were applicable to me at that time, a master's degree holder with six years of professional experience. I started getting shortlisted for interviews and getting offers.

But not all offers are as good as what we want them to be. And I was not even being picky back then. My only criterion was that the offer should be higher than what I was getting back home, and I thought that was an easy criterion to meet (no offence to my home country).

There were laughable offers from physiotherapy clinics with desperate proprietors who wanted to employ me right away so they would have a physiotherapy professional with a master's degree. They were *not* even hiring me for a physiotherapy staff position to begin with. They were offering me a clerical position because I didn't have my UAE licence to practise physiotherapy yet.

They said that in the meantime, I could work in the reception area. The offer amounted to half of what I was already earning in the Philippines, and they promised to increase my pay and promote me as a physiotherapy staff as soon as I had my licence.

According to the person who interviewed me, they were in a hurry to sign me up because they were about to undergo an audit, and they needed more staff with a master's degree. They were trying to lock me in while lowballing me at the same time.

They were capitalising on the fact that I was on a tourist visa at the time, and they were hoping I would be desperate to take their offer, so I did not have to go home empty-handed. The same thing happened at two other clinics too.

And that is why I consider it a privilege to be able to say *no* to job offers knowing that you deserve a better one. It basically boils down to not giving in to the fear of not having any job at all.

We would all be less desperate if we would simply take time to reflect and assure ourselves of our worth. If an employer says no to you, it just means *no for them* right now. It means what you are looking for is not a good fit with what they are looking for right now.

You'd be surprised by the number of people who are suffering from thinking they are not enough. I, too have suffered from this syndrome, more often than I care to admit. But it is a privilege to wake up some days knowing that *I'm enough*, a mantra I learned from a childhood friend. You too, are enough! Let that sink in.

A day before flying back to the Philippines after my two-month vacation in Dubai, I got an interview at a government institution in Abu Dhabi. They were planning to start offering a physiotherapy program for female students and they would need lecturers for the upcoming academic year.

After the interview, I flew back home to the Philippines with a good feeling in my heart. It took three months to hear from them again, but the wait time was all worth it. It was the best offer among all prospective employers I had, and it was so worth it not having said yes to all those previous offers.

What if I had been wrong? What if they hadn't hired me? Then it would have been life as usual for me: continuing my work in the Philippines. This still does not refute the fact that it really is a privilege to be able to say no.

Don't get me wrong, I didn't see anything inherently wrong with doing a clerical job while I worked my way into the role I wanted. But had I taken one of the earlier offers, knowing myself, I wouldn't have been able to discover this path towards financial freedom and be on this personal finance journey of becoming and keeping myself debt-free.

I DON'T FEAR THE CONCEPT OF WANTING MORE MONEY

It's a privilege to be unapologetic about wanting more money. I'm quite sure we all have heard the infamous saying that *"money is the root of all evil"*. At a very young age, we were taught to appreciate and put more importance on non-earthly possessions because they are more virtuous than having plenty of money.

We have been led to believe that wanting or needing a lot of money is bad and selfish. So, the result is we shy away from admitting we'd prefer to have more money than we have right now, because we might look selfish, ungodly, or evil.

But isn't it more sensible to think that the lack of money is the root of evil? If you don't have enough money, it gets harder to fulfil your needs, which could lead to putting you in a rough spot. And we all know what a desperate person in a rough spot can do!

Let us look at Abraham Maslow's hierarchy of needs[1] where it shows the needs that require urgent fulfilment (at the bottom of the triangle) and those that can be fulfilled later (higher levels).

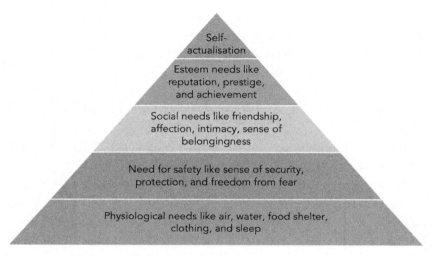

Self-actualisation

Esteem needs like reputation, prestige, and achievement

Social needs like friendship, affection, intimacy, sense of belongingness

Need for safety like sense of security, protection, and freedom from fear

Physiological needs like air, water, food shelter, clothing, and sleep

Figure 3. Abraham Maslow's hierarchy of needs

In our modern society, every single thing costs money. Based on Maslow's hierarchy of needs, at the lowest level alone, only air and sleep are free. But even sleep requires a place to do it, and the place requires money.

If you're consistently in a situation wherein you don't have enough money for food, water, clothes, a roof above your head, then you enter a state of desperation which could lead you to do things you would not normally do if you had enough money.

So, no, money is not the root of all evil. It is a requirement in this day and age. It is what will make us decent, modest, nourished, protected, warm and alive. How could something that does all those things be evil?

Personal finance guru Ramit Sethi requires his clients to define their *rich life* at the outset. He encourages them not to be ashamed or hold back in their declarations as to what a rich life means to them. I actually agree with this mindset.

If you think it is wrong to covet something in life, then you might find it disagreeable to live a life in our modern society. Capitalism makes a lot of things possible for us that we couldn't have imagined we could ever experience decades or centuries ago.

I can't farm my own food and grow my own meat right now, but I can earn money by getting a job or building a business, and then I can pay someone else to source the food for me (i.e., grocery stores).

I don't have time to sew my own clothes right now, but I can earn money, and pay someone else to make clothes for me (i.e., clothes shops).

If you picture your rich life as being able to buy ketchup, toothpaste, or any food and consumable items without having to sift through the brands to find the cheapest, then wanting money to fulfil that is not evil at all.

MY VILLAGE'S BUY-IN

It takes a village to be debt-free, but it starts with you. The journey towards being debt-free can be really daunting. Whenever you look at your numbers, it feels as though it is not doable. Whenever you check your timeline, it seems as though that time will never come. But you are not alone, and in time it becomes doable and exciting.

It goes without saying that my journey towards being debt-free was made easier by the fantastic people around me. I didn't have to announce my journey nor broadcast every single milestone. In fact, everything was extremely private, just between me and my trusty spreadsheet. But because of my people's "buy-in" to my lifestyle choices, it made the journey much smoother.

With my friends and family, I considered them not judging my very basic style as their buy-in. I didn't have to worry about not having the latest kicks or the trendiest clothes at all. In a way, if you are with the right company, you really don't feel that fear of missing out.

I'm grateful for their patience with me whenever I suggested going out to try out this food or that experience without having to break the bank. Although I'm pretty sure they liked that idea too!

My biggest thanks go to my partner whose buy-in is shown through his constant tolerance of my need to always balance my spreadsheet down to the last centavo (I do not balance my spreadsheet down to the last centavo anymore. I have a better way that doesn't require me to always look at my spreadsheet. More on that in a later chapter.), and his acceptance of the fact that I'm his polar opposite when it comes to spending. As I have mentioned in Chapter 2, he is the more adventurous one between the two of us, and almost all adventure costs money.

I'm grateful he understands that I don't want to spend money on various activities I'll only be doing once, just to say that I have tried it. I want to spend on experiences I consider meaningful and that I'll be doing more than once and possibly indefinitely.

I appreciate he understands I don't want to spend on a lot on material things because I only want to splurge on a few items that are dear to me. And even though we have completely different money habits – which compelled us to manage our money separately – thank goodness we never fight about it. It could also be possible that we don't fight about it because we manage our money separately.

Nevertheless, I'm thankful to him because without his buy-in, we wouldn't be able to make this unconventional financial household situation work.

I also consider it a privilege to not have anyone within my inner circle who would influence me poorly about how I manage my money. My mother has a very good (perhaps tight would be a better word) grasp on managing household money, as is evidenced by my stories in Chapter 2.

My sister has also been a good influence on me when it comes to personal finance, being that her double-income household of a family of five is completely debt-free.

As for my close friends, we don't really talk about personal finance per se, but from my point of view as a person looking from the outside, I don't think any one of them is swimming in consumer debt right now.

However, I do meet new people every once in a while who aren't really good role models when it comes to personal finance, and meeting them makes me all the more grateful that I lucked out on having good money influences from within my inner circle.

I remember during my first year in the UAE, I met someone who kept on telling me to buy designer bags, accessories, shoes, etc. She kept telling me that with my kind of salary, I could easily afford them. No matter her insistence, I wouldn't budge.

At some point, I even told her I'd rather put the money towards buying more stocks or keeping it in case I would need extra money for the construction of my building (at that time, my apartment complex back home was still at its planning stage).

She told me I didn't need to do such things. I didn't need to concern myself with such financial matters of securing my future through entrepreneurship and investment. She was adamant that because I'm a woman, the man – she meant my future husband because I was single back then – should be responsible for providing me a secure future.

I was taken aback by her statement. I thought I'd been transported back to a time when women were the "property" of men, and a woman didn't have the freedom to own a property, let alone earn her own money and be financially secure through her own efforts.

I blinked at her statement and realised I was still in the 21st century, and I had literally heard her advice a few seconds earlier. Even now, I can't remember how I responded to her advice. It is possible I may not have responded at all. That was how flabbergasted I was!

From that point forward, I swore to myself to be selective with the financial advice I would take from friends, and that unsolicited advice should be totally ignored.

Don't worry, I didn't unfriend her because of that comment. I still see her from time to time. She is still my friend anyway. She still likes adorning herself with luxury items, designer handbags, clothes and footwear, at her husband's expense (she does not work anymore).

Recognising your privilege lessens the likelihood that you'll continue giving excuse after excuse to avoid getting out of debt and resigning yourself to a life of "mountains of debt are normal". Don't let "debt is normal" become your mantra.

SECTION THREE
KEEPING YOUR DEBT-FREE STATUS

In this third part of the book, we are going to dive into various strategies that you may consider as you secure your journey towards keeping yourself or your household debt-free. If you are at this phase in your personal finance journey, congratulations! You have done the hardest part: being debt-free! Getting off the debt train is no easy feat. Staying debt-free is another matter.

If you chance upon strategies in this section that you have already been utilising in your personal finance management, bravo! Getting to know that you have already been using a strategy long before being aware others have been highly recommending it, gives you a nod of approval, a proverbial two-thumbs up that lets you know you are moving in the right direction.

This section also includes personal reflections on how these strategies became my lifesaver amidst a sea of uncertainties in managing my personal finances. Feel free to apply one, two, or all the strategies, whatever works for you. There are numerous other strategies out there – I have created a list of books that I highly recommend for further reading about other money strategies – but I have only included in this section strategies I have adopted in my own personal finance management that have allowed me to enjoy my life while being financially secure and staying debt-free along the way. I only hope my favourite strategies work for you too.

Figure 4, below, shows the third phase highlighted in bold as I dedicate the next three chapters to talking about what I do to keep my finances in check and maintain my debt-free status.

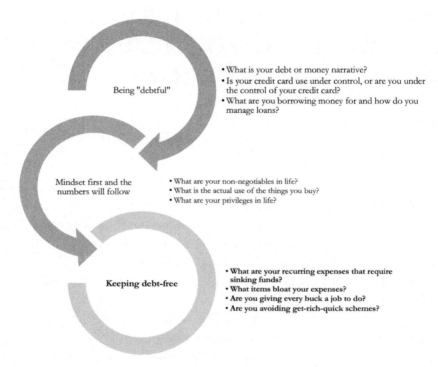

Figure 4. An overview of the reflective approach that guided my debt-free journey, with the focus on keeping debt-free

CHAPTER 7

CREATE SINKING FUNDS FOR RECURRING EXPENSES AND LIFE PROJECTS

C reating sinking funds for recurring life projects and possible financial emergencies is a game-changer. It is like having free money to spend when you need it the most. Or having free money to buy the thing or pay for the experience that you want at the time that you need it.

Imagine the concept of 0% easy payment plan offered by your credit cards, or much simpler, the concept of Tabby, Afterpay, or any of those buy now, pay later schemes. You make a purchase now and you pay it off in instalments for the next 3, 6, 12 or 24 months. Try to picture that in reverse and you've got yourself a sinking fund!

What are the things you need to set up for your sinking funds? Your bank account should allow for opening an e-savings account separate to your regular current account. Preferably, you must be able to open one account for each sinking fund you want to create.

These e-savings accounts do not have debit cards connected to them, so taking out money on a whim is discouraged right away. Of course, you can conveniently transfer money from your e-savings to your current account so you can withdraw money when you need to, but the act of separating them gives you proper accounting of your sinking funds.

It would also be nice if you are banking with an institution that gives high interest rates for savings accounts or monthly bonus rates if you deposit money into it at least once a month and do not make any withdrawals in that same month.

A lot of banks have this savings account scheme with varying features and names (e.g., rewards saver, iSaver, etc.), but for the purpose of setting up our sinking funds, we need two simple but very important features: (1) the money is separate from our debit account and (2) the accounts earn interest.

The good thing about sinking funds is that they will earn you a couple of hundred bucks more while the money is sitting in a high yield savings account. It is like a small-scale version of the common saying in the financial world: *"Make your money work for you."*

If your bank does not have this feature or allows for only a limited number of e-savers, then you can open one separate high yield savings account, put all your savings in there regardless of which sinking fund they should go to, and monitor how much goes into each sinking fund using your budget spreadsheet. This will allow you to keep your sinking funds separate from your easy-to-access current account and away from easy withdrawal.

If this seems tedious, you can go with the old school practice of using money envelopes wherein you dedicate an envelope for each sinking fund you are setting up. Each pay day, withdraw from your current account the money you need to put in each money envelope. The only problem with this method is it will not earn you any interest on your savings.

I can only give examples about how I used sinking funds to my advantage, but ultimately, you will be the one to identify what your sinking funds are going to be for. If you did a reflection of your non-negotiables after reading Chapter 4, and if those non-negotiables require funds that you need to accumulate over time, then you would already know what you will need your sinking funds for.

If you still haven't processed and reflected on what you truly desire, then take all the time you need to sort this out. Since that deed is paradigm shifting, in that you will need to stop acquiring things and experiences that you do not derive satisfaction from in order to find what you truly desire, it might take some time.

For now, allow me to share my experiences on where I use sinking funds in my life.

SINKING FUND FOR THE NEXT TRIP

As I have mentioned in an earlier chapter, travelling is one of my non-negotiables in life right now. As of writing, I have travelled to over 30 countries. But I have only employed the use of sinking funds to my latter trips.

Before, I used to book a flight a few months prior to my intended trip, charge it to my credit card and pay it off. By the time my travel date came round, I used my credit card again for all my travel expenses and paid them off once I returned from my trip, from the salary I would be receiving that month.

So, with that short narrative, you can already see the flaw in my budgeting for that month. It was like I was operating on a devil-may-care budget during those months of high expense.

Because I was working as a college lecturer during my time in the UAE, I would only have the opportunity to travel when the schools were closed: spring break, summer break, or winter break. And then there were those long public holiday weekends when I would try to squeeze in a short trip to a nearby European country. These brief trips were usually unplanned and booked at the last minute.

Nevertheless, it does not matter whether your trip is planned or unplanned. If you don't earmark a portion of your salary towards travel (or whatever your *non-negotiables in life* are), you'll always end up with an erratic monthly budget, just like I did when I wasn't using the concept of sinking funds yet.

I used to end up blowing through my income for certain months of the year (March–April during spring break, July–August during summer break, December during winter break) just because I didn't plan financially well for the trips.

Not to mention the small trips I took during long public holiday weekends. Even though they were shorter trips and generally cheaper than travelling on a spring break, summer break, or winter break, they still put a little dent in my budgeting if not properly taken care of.

To simplify the application of a sinking fund to save for a trip, I will use my central Europe trip as an example. It was a two-week trip that I took during one of my winter breaks (December). At the start of that year, I knew I wanted to take a trip in December. At that time, I hadn't figured out where to go yet. All I knew was that I wanted to travel for the entire two weeks of my winter break.

I decided to save AED 1,000 (~USD 270) per month from January to November. I opened an e-savings account and labelled it "Travel". By the end of October that year, when I finally decided where I wanted to travel, I booked a flight and applied for a Schengen visa. Of course, this cost money, which presumably would have inflated my spending for that month if I hadn't had my sinking fund.

By then, I already had AED 10,000 (~USD 2,720) in my travel sinking fund. And even though I used my credit card to purchase my plane ticket and apply for my visa, I instantly paid those off from my travel sinking fund.

At the time of the trip, I had more than enough to cover my expenses while travelling through four different countries. It was more than enough, so I had a few hundred dirhams left from my travel sinking fund after I settled all my expenses.

What did I feel after that trip regarding my personal finance management?

- Call me dramatic but it felt liberating because I was able to collect awesome memories during that trip and I didn't even have to go into debt to gain so much. The whole trip felt like it was paid for by someone else, all because I didn't have to use a good chunk of my salary that month to pay for it.
- I didn't feel deprived in any way during the trip. Before, there was always that nagging feeling at the back of my mind telling me to check if I'd been overspending during my trip or not. It felt amazing to not have to think about budgeting during that trip, because I knew I had the money for it.

- I felt like a very responsible adult who had it all figured out. Of course, I do *not* have it all figured out, so please do not misquote me on that. But it was nice to feel that way having accomplished one of my *non-negotiables in life* without owing anything to the big financial corporations.

SINKING FUND FOR ANNUAL INSURANCE PREMIUMS

Annual insurance premiums could be any of the following: car insurance, renter's insurance, homeowners' insurance, disability insurance, or health insurance – that is, if your employer does not provide one.

Perhaps, all of these apply to you, or perhaps none at all. There are more types of insurance out there, but it is not within the scope of this book to discuss each and every one of them.

Nevertheless, purchasing an insurance policy for your car, the property you're renting, your own home, or your health insurance is not a small matter, and therefore must be prepared for. For this sinking fund, let us use my health insurance sinking fund as an example.

Prior to my sabbatical year, health insurance was one of the things I made a sinking fund for. I knew that not being sponsored by an employer during that year meant I had to source my own health insurance while staying in the UAE.

Since my golden visa was under the sponsorship of Abu Dhabi, I needed to prepare myself to pay a hefty price for my health insurance alone. The cheapest insurance policy for Abu Dhabi residents as of writing was at least AED 3,000 (~USD 820), and that was the most basic policy without any add-ons.

I really wanted one with a few add-ons that were quite beneficial to me, such as dental and optical (I change eyeglasses every year because I'm 5.00+ "blind"). After careful consideration and extensive research, I settled on a health insurance policy priced at AED 4,100 (~USD 1,120) per annum.

How much did my sinking fund for health insurance policy have at the time of purchase? I had AED 6,000 (~USD 1,630) waiting in there, from the AED 500 (~USD 140) that I saved each month from January to December 2022. I was able to buy the health insurance policy that was most beneficial for me without worrying about the price. I even had change! It is like getting free money when you least expect it.

You might say, *"But it is your own money anyway, so it is not free money."* While you are technically correct, just remember all those times when you checked your jeans or trouser pockets before you put them in the washing machine, and you suddenly see a spare 10, 20, or 50 bucks you never thought you had. That was how I felt with my extra AED 1,900 (~USD 510) from my health insurance sinking fund after I purchased what I ultimately needed for a policy.

SINKING FUND FOR OPTICAL, DENTAL, OR OTHER HEALTH-RELATED PROCEDURES

Following a sinking fund for health insurance as an example, not all of us might have access to health insurance policies that have optical and dental as add-ons, especially if our health insurance is provided by employers that do not give options to employees to pay for add-ons out of their own pocket. And even if we are given the freedom to pay for our own insurance add-ons, the benefits might not be enough to cover what we really need.

For example, even if my health insurance policy allows me to purchase eyeglasses once each year, it has never been enough to cover the total amount. I have had years when my optical coverage from my employer was AED 1,000 (~USD 270) and years when it was only AED 500 (~USD 140), and even years without!

Due to strong prescriptions for my near-sightedness and astigmatism, my specific requirements for high-index lenses alone usually cost me a few thousand bucks, without the frames yet.

Similarly, with dental procedures, we might need to pay more than what our insurance benefits could cover. If, per professional advice, we need to undergo at least one prophylactic treatment every six months (more if we have recurrent dental and gum problems) and the insurance coverage for these sessions are enough, then great!

But if our dentist advises us to undergo more than the routine cleaning and simple filling, then we might be out of pocket by a huge amount, especially if it involves dental surgery.

The best antidote to these erratic – or lack of – benefits and coverage is to set up a sinking fund for your optical and dental benefit add-ons.

This might not even have to be about optical or dental procedures. Are you planning to undergo an elective surgery soon? Open a sinking fund for it!

Let us even go wider and include your expenses that augment your general well-being. Do you like massages and cannot go a week without them? Go ahead and start a sinking fund for your massage and other spa treatments. Every time you dip into that fund, it feels like you are getting "free" massages.

Are you eyeing up a cosmetic procedure that will help you gain a healthier sense of self, whatever that means to you? Go ahead and put your savings for that procedure in a separate sinking fund.

Regardless of your reason for opening this particular sinking fund, the main objective remains the same. Opening a sinking fund dedicated to health-related expenses will surely help you avoid or alleviate debt should the need for any expensive medical interventions arise.

In certain countries, there are what they call health savings accounts (HSAs) and flexible savings accounts (FSAs) that allow eligible individuals to save money which they can use for out-of-pocket medical expenses not usually covered by their health insurance. Check out if these accounts are available in your country. It would be nice to have one in lieu of this sinking fund because HSAs and FSAs are tax-advantaged accounts.

SINKING FUND FOR RENT

We always set aside a certain portion of our salary for rent. But do we really need a sinking fund for something as mundane as rent? My answer to this is a resounding yes.

Whether your rent is due weekly, bi-weekly, or monthly, you can definitely benefit from keeping your rent in a separate sinking fund. It ensures this is not mixed up with all your other financial commitments.

This will likely ensure you do not go, *"Oh, I thought I still had money for that"* or, *"I'm sure I set aside that rent money"* and be disappointed by the lack of it come payment time. If your salary is paid more often than your rent payment due dates, then all the more that this sinking fund is for you.

For example, if you receive your salary weekly but your rent is not due until the end of each month, you are better off building that monthly rent from the salary you receive each week.

When I lived in Abu Dhabi and Dubai for almost ten years, my rent was either paid in two cheques (every six months) or four cheques (every quarter) for a year's rent. Imagine how much money I should have had in my bank account during those months when my cheques needed to clear.

Prior to my coming to the UAE, I learned that UAE landlords ask for one cheque for the entire year's rent. Fortunately, the rent payment scheme has become more favourable for tenants as the years have gone by.

As of writing, it is not uncommon to see landlords and property managers asking for six cheques (every two months).

The option to pay rent monthly is becoming popular as well (a payment scheme that has been long common among those who room-share, too).

As an example, let us look at how I built up my sinking fund for a four-cheque annual rent of AED 72,600 (~USD 19,770) a year. Thankfully, when I moved to that property, it was January, which will make our example of quarterly payment much easier to illustrate.

Table 2. Applying the sinking fund concept to save for quarterly rent

Rent due on	Amount of cheque (rent due, in AED)	Amount I take out from my salary each month to build my sinking fund for quarterly rent (in AED)		
21st of Jan[a]	18,150[b]	6,050[c] from my Oct salary	6,050 from my Nov salary	6,050 from my Dec salary
21st of Apr	18,150	6,050 from my Jan salary	6,050 from my Feb salary	6,050 from my Mar salary
21st of Jul	18,150	6,050 from my Apr salary	6,050 from my May salary	6,050 from my Jun salary
21st of Oct	18,150	6,050 from my Jul salary	6,050 from my Aug salary	6,050 from my Sep salary

[a] The payment scheme always requires tenants to clear the first cheque before moving in.

[b] AED 18,150 is ~USD 4,940

[c] AED 6,050 is ~USD 1,650

As you can see from Table 2, I didn't wait for my January's salary to be able to pay that AED 18,150 (~USD 4,940) quarterly rent. I made sure I started putting away this amount three months prior.

Now, on your first year of moving to a new property, since tenants are required to clear the first cheque before moving in, it would seem you would only need to put up money for the remaining three quarters of the year.

Using the same example above, with a total rent of AED 72,600 (~USD 19,770) per year, paying AED 18,150 (~USD 4,940) in full prior to moving means you are left only with AED 54,450 (~USD 14,820) to pay for the whole year's rent.

Mathematically speaking, you only need to tuck away AED 6,050 (~USD 1,650) from your salaries from January to March to pay for the *April quarterly rent*, April to June for your *July rent*, and July to September for your *October rent*. Which means you have a huge spending space from October to December (see the greyed out portion of Table 2) that year since your whole year's rent is paid already! Right?

Technically, yes. But that practice is wrong! Do not make the mistake of stopping putting money in this sinking fund as soon as you have paid that year's rent in full, unless you plan on being homeless for the first quarter of next year.

Now, let us look at alternative scenarios wherein the landlord would require me to pay rent every two months and every six months. Tables 3 and 4 show my would-be sinking fund scheme for six cheques and two cheques, respectively, based on the same total annual rent of AED 72,600 (~USD 19,770).

Table 3. Applying the sinking fund concept to save for bi-monthly rent

Rent due on	Amount of cheque (rent due, in AED)	Amount I take out from my salary each month to build my sinking fund for bi-monthly rent (in AED)	
21st of Jan	12,100[a]	6,050[b] (Nov)	6,050 (Dec)
21st of Mar	12,100	6,050 (Jan)	6,050 (Feb)
21st of May	12,100	6,050 (Mar)	6,050 (Apr)
21st of Jul	12,100	6,050 (May)	6,050 (Jun)
21st of Sep	12,100	6,050 (Jul)	6,050 (Aug)
21st of Nov	12,100	6,050 (Sep)	6,050 (Oct)

[a] AED 12,100 is ~USD 3,290
[b] AED 6,050 is ~USD 1,650

Table 4. Applying the sinking fund concept to save for semi-annual rent

Rent due on	Amount of cheque (rent due, in AED)	Amount I take out from my salary each month to build my sinking fund for semi-annual rent (in AED)					
21st of Jan	36,300[a]	6,050[b] (Jul)	6,050 (Aug)	6,050 (Sep)	6,050 (Oct)	6,050 (Nov)	6,050 (Dec)
21st of Jul	36,300	6,050 (Jan)	6,050 (Feb)	6,050 (Mar)	6,050 (Apr)	6,050 (May)	6,050 (Jun)

[a] AED 36,300 is ~USD 9,880
[b] AED 6,050 is ~USD 1,650

Now, even if the above payment scheme examples are not applicable to your situation and even if you pay your rent monthly as you receive your monthly salary, there is no reason not to set up a sinking fund related to rent.

Remember, if and when you move to another property, almost always, security deposit and property manager fees are required. Not to mention the cost of paying movers, new furniture to fill in a bigger property if you're upsizing, and new appliances if you're upgrading some of your old ones from the old home. That big surge of expense is best mitigated with a full sinking fund just waiting to be used when the need arises.

SINKING FUND FOR EMERGENCY FUND

An emergency fund is a fund that individuals or households can use without penalty in case of an emergency.[1] It's too formal right? In J.L. Collins' book *The Simple Path to Wealth*, he refers to this fund as "F-you money". He sets it up so he can secure his freedom of not being tied down to a job he doesn't want or having to work for a boss he doesn't want to work for anymore.

Call it emergency fund, F-you money, or whatever you want, the more important thing is to actually have one!

Left and right, there is still a debate as to how much a household should have in an emergency fund. But the most common advice is between three months' or six months' worth of expenses.

So, for your own situation, how much money do you really require in your emergency fund? To help you answer this question, let us dig deeper into the bases of recommendations relating to emergency funds.

Losing one's job is one big life emergency. If you suddenly lost your job right now, would you be able to cover all your expenses for the current month? How about for the next month? How long could you sustain your current standard of living after losing your job?

You might say, it does not matter how long because you can find another job anyway. Then I guess the right question is, how long until you find a new job?

In the 1990s, the average length of unemployment was three months. Hence, three months' worth of emergency funds[2] became the common guideline. Basing the stamina of one's emergency fund on a typical length of unemployment seems quite a straightforward formula: no income, take it out from the emergency fund.

Studies in the 2000s, however, found that the increase in the length of unemployment consequently required an increase in emergency fund stamina, which led to the recommendation of five[3] to six[4] months' worth of emergency fund.

The average period of unemployment continually changes, is cyclical, and longer during a recession. Therefore, it is best to do a quick search on your own to feel the current economic climate.

When I started working, I didn't have an emergency fund myself. In a peer-reviewed article published in 2022, overconfidence resulted in people underestimating the need for an emergency fund.[5] And they're right, because in my head, I thought I never really needed one. I relied on the liquid assets that I had (e.g., stocks, mutual funds) to keep me afloat should I ever lose my job or leave it voluntarily while not having a lead for a next job.

Before I moved from the Philippines to the UAE, I didn't work for six months. I relentlessly used my credit card for my basic needs and travel (as I have mentioned in Chapter 2) because I didn't want to disrupt the growth of my stocks. If I'd sold them, then I'd have lost that investment opportunity.

So, I deliberately chose to be in debt during those six months rather than touch my liquid assets. In hindsight, I could have done more to prepare myself for that period of my life. I failed to adequately predict my emergency needs and next move in life, so much so that I somehow ended up in massive debt.

Back then, my knowledge about emergency funds was oversimplistic. I thought my stocks and mutual funds were sufficient to rely on, only to end up not wanting to use them in that time of "emergency".

Emergency funds can be categorised into three: quick, intermediate and comprehensive. *Quick funds* refer to what is inside your current and savings accounts. *Intermediate funds* comprise your quick funds plus any long-term savings (e.g., certificates of deposit). *Comprehensive funds* are your quick and intermediate funds, plus stocks, bonds and mutual funds, minus the retirement account.[6]

My mistake was that I was high on stocks and mutual funds, but my checking and savings accounts didn't have much. With my mindset of not touching my stocks and mutual funds when the need arose, it was as if I didn't have any emergency funds at all.

More often than not, a person or household's emergency fund, whether three months' worth or six months' worth, is usually kept in a high yield savings account. Once you complete your emergency fund, it feels quite good to know it is there in that high yield savings account, ready to be accessed anytime. Plus, it earns while it sits there.

But do not forget that there is an opportunity cost if you let a huge amount of money idly sit in a high yield savings account when you could invest part of it. This is the very reason why the categories of emergency fund mentioned above make a lot of sense.

A large amount of money left as quick funds (current and savings account) is not inflation-proof. Therefore, distribute your emergency fund carefully into the three categories mentioned above.

Have enough so you can quickly take it when the need arises, and also, do not put all your emergency funds into stocks, bonds and mutual funds such that you would think twice and be hesitant in liquidating it when you need it.

Is it possible to not need to put up an emergency fund? Yes. In what situations will you not need this emergency fund? When you have extensive investments and when you have high job security (e.g., tenured university lecturers).

For the former, having extensive investments means more income streams, which is an excellent mitigator for having access to credit should you lose your job right now. For the latter, having high job security is self-explanatory. There is no foreseeable future when you would likely lose your job.

Despite job security however, it is best to keep in mind that no employee is completely indispensable. A health problem (yours or someone you care for) might lead to an indefinite leave, which your employer might see as detrimental to your job.

You have a job because your employer needs you. Regardless of whether you are the best person in the world to do the job you are doing right now and you are promised of employment forever, if you are unfit to do that job, you will likely lose it.

Hence, if you rely on your job as your *sole* income stream and you are not prepared to lose it (i.e., you do not have an emergency fund) then you are likely to go broke. There is only a fine thread of lifeline keeping you from being broke and that is your job. Keep that in mind.

SINKING FUND FOR GIFTS

Notice that during the holidays, gift giving is rampant which leads to a more than usual level of consumption during those days or months. During the first quarter of every year, a lot of people are still recovering from their massive expenses accumulated during Christmas and New Year's celebrations.

It goes without saying that not planning for such events will really throw a spanner into your budget plan. It is much easier to buy gifts for the holidays (and birthdays) if you already have an earmarked fund for this.

By now, you already know what the first step is: open a separate e-savings account for this sinking fund and label it "Gifts".

For the purpose of showing an example of sinking funds for massive gift giving, I will use the Christmas holiday as an example. This means that December is going to be an expensive month for us gift-giving-wise.

Go over your gift expenses for Christmas in the last three years. Add them up and take the average. Suppose that you spent AED 12,000 (~USD 3,270) for Christmas gifts three years ago, AED 10,000 (~USD 2,720) two years ago, and AED 11,000 (~USD 2,990) last year. Taking the average of this yields AED 11,000 (~USD 2,990). Let us use this number then to create our sinking fund schedule for our Christmas gifts.

We definitely do not want to take all that AED 11,000 (~USD 2,990) from our December salary, or risk ourselves paying it all off in January or February of the next year. It is best to spread it out evenly and start saving from January of the same year.

Divide AED 11,000 (~USD 2,990) by 11 months (January to November) which is equal to AED 1,000 (~USD 270) per month. We have to have the total amount by November so we can spend it in December, hence, splitting it up into 11 instances only.

If you want to include December, split the total into 12 instances, keeping in mind that what you save for December has already started your fund for next year's Christmas.

For birthdays, list the names of all the people you intend to give birthday gifts to in a given year. Group them according to their birth month.

Provide a budget for each of them. I'm pretty sure that not all the people on our to-gift list are equal in our eyes and there are some who will definitely receive a more special gift than the rest. I'm just being realistic here (we all have *our inner circle friends*) and I'm only giving this reminder to ensure you peg the right amount for your gift-giving budget and avoid being short.

Once you have assigned each person a gift amount, add up the total cost for each month. In my circle of people, September is the month with the greatest number of birthday celebrators. Let us use this month as an example.

Table 5. A sample schedule of birthday celebrators and your intended gift amount for each person

Name	Birthday	Gift amount (in AED)
Lisa	2 September	250[a]
Eric	12 September	250
John	12 September	250
Carla (bestie)	14 September	500[b]
Daphne	25 September	250
September total		1,500[c]

[a] AED 250 is ~USD 70

[b] AED 500 is ~USD 140

[c] AED 1,500 is ~USD 410

For me to buy these gifts, I have to make sure I have the total amount by August, NOT September. If I do not have the total amount tucked away by August, my September budget might be ruined. You might say, *"But then my August budget might also be ruined because not every month, I would need to spend this much on birthday gifts."* Okay, I hear you. Let us make a plan for the entire year then.

Table 6. A sample schedule of a sinking fund for birthday gifts for a year, using a constant amount of contribution each month

Month	Gift expenditure per month (in AED)	Sinking fund outstanding balance (in AED)
January	250[a]	0 + **500** – 250 = 250
February	500[b]	250 + **500** – 500 = 250
March	250	250 + **500** – 250 = 500
April	500	500 + **500** – 500 = 500
May	0	500 + **500** – 0 = 1,000[d]
June	250	1,000 + **500** – 250 = 1,250[e]
July	500	1,250 + **500** – 500 = 1,250
August	250	1,250 + **500** – 250 = 1,500[f]
September	1,500	1,500 + **500** – 1,500 = 500
October	500	500 + **500** – 500 = 500
November	750[c]	500 + **500** – 750 = 250
December	750	250 + **500** – 750 = 0
Total	6,000[g]	

[a] AED 250 is ~USD 70
[b] AED 500 is ~USD 140
[c] AED 750 is ~USD 200
[d] AED 1,000 is ~USD 270
[e] AED 1,250 is ~USD 340
[f] AED 1,500 is ~USD 410
[g] AED 6,000 is ~USD 1,630

In the year-long example in Table 6 above, each month has a different gift amount total shown in the second column. Adding them all up, we have AED 6,000 (~USD 1,630) for the whole year. Dividing this total by 12 months to make a fixed monthly contribution will yield AED 500 (~USD 140).

In the third column, starting with 0 in this fund, we keep adding AED 500 (in bold) (~USD 140) each month. We take out the gift amount we need for that month (third figure of third column) and we are left with the difference (fourth figure of third column). What is left is then rolled over to the new contribution next month. We repeat this until we get the entire year's calculation, ensuring we will not have any short months.

You can also do it by starting with the biggest amount you have, and then rolling over what is left onto the next month. From the same example above, we know that your highest total gift amount in a given month is that of September amounting to AED 1,500 (~USD 410). So, let us start with that amount. Each month, the goal is to keep the gift fund up to AED 1,500 before taking out the gift amount.

Table 7. A sample schedule of a sinking fund for birthday gifts for a year, keeping a constant amount of AED 1,500 in the fund

Month	Gift expenditure per month (in AED)	Sinking fund outstanding balance (in AED)
January	250[a]	0 + **1,500** − 250 = 1,250
February	500[b]	1,250 + **250** − 500 = 1,000[d]
March	250	1,000 + **500** − 250 = 1,250[e]
April	500	1,250 + **250** − 500 = 1,000
May	0	1,000 + **500** − 0 = 1,500[f]
June	250	1,000 + **500** − 250 = 1,250
July	500	1,250 + **250** − 500 = 1,000
August	250	1,000 + **500** − 250 = 1,250
September	1,500	1,250 + **250** − 1,500 = 0
October	500	0 + **1,500** − 500 = 1,000
November	750[c]	1,000 + **500** − 750 = 750
December	750	750 − 750 = 0
Total	6,000[g]	

[a] AED 250 is ~USD 70
[b] AED 500 is ~USD 140
[c] AED 750 is ~USD 200
[d] AED 1,000 is ~USD 270
[e] AED 1,250 is ~USD 340
[f] AED 1,500 is ~USD 410
[g] AED 6,000 is ~USD 1,630

Choosing any of the allotment schemes above can do wonders for your budget. You can avoid fluctuations in your budget and the surprise of inflated spending during holidays, when most of our gift-shopping happens.

Those, so far, are the sinking funds I have right now. But what else can I use sinking funds for in the future? I've also been applying the sinking fund concept to prepare for bigger purchases like a car or probably a house. Let us take a look at how we can do this.

SINKING FUND FOR A DEPOSIT OR DOWN PAYMENT

I know you've been waiting for this recommendation since we talked about preparing for big-ticket purchases like buying a property or a car in Chapter 3. Remember, I discouraged you from applying for a mortgage or car financing with less than a 20% down payment because it becomes more expensive in the long run, plus the lack of equity right from the start of the loan. So here it is. Let's dive deeper into how we can prepare much better for these big-ticket purchases.

Same as any of the other sinking funds we have discussed earlier, create a separate e-saver account for this fund. Make sure it earns interest because among all your sinking funds, this one will definitely have the highest average daily balance and you'll want to optimise the earnings on that through its interest rate. Sometimes, some banks even give out bonus interest if you do not withdraw from the same account within a month. Look up what's applicable in your country.

For a property

Calculate your 20% down payment based on the price of the property you are aiming for. There is always an average price for housing based on its size (e.g., studio, one-bedroom flat, two-bedroom townhouse, three-bedroom single-detached, etc.) and location (i.e., some cities, towns, or suburbs have pricier homes than others).

Do your research and keep in mind what we have learned in the non-negotiables in life and utilitarian premise chapters of this book (Chapters 4 and 5 respectively). In this example, let us use AED 1,000,000 (~USD 272,260) as the base price of the property you aim to buy. This would mean that you would need at least AED 200,000 (~USD 54,450) saved up.

I say "at least" because you would definitely want to make sure you have enough to cover the other costs of purchasing a property. These costs include, but are not limited to, government fees, agency fees, service fees, mortgage fees, inspection fees, all on top of your property down payment.

Considering all these, let us make our target amount AED 250,000

(~USD 68,060) instead. If there are two of you working and earning in a household (i.e., usually both the spouses), then you can decide from these two options:

1. Scheme A: put the entire amount of one of your salaries into the sinking fund and use the other's salary for your household's living costs, or
2. Scheme B: equally divide the amount you would each put into the sinking fund.

Table 8. Sample Scheme A dedicating one spouse's salary into the sinking fund for a property down payment (and extras)

Sinking fund for property down payment and extras	Spouse 1's monthly salary	Spouse 2's monthly salary
AED 250,000[a]	AED 25,000[b]	AED 25,000
Contributions	Spouse 1's monthly contribution (in AED)	Spouse 2's monthly contribution (in AED)
Month 1	25,000	0 (spouse 2's monthly salary is used for living costs)
Month 2	25,000	0
Month 3	25,000	0
Month 4	25,000	0
Month 5	25,000	0
Month 6	25,000	0
Month 7	25,000	0
Month 8	25,000	0
Month 9	25,000	0
Month 10	25,000	0
Total	AED 250,000	0

[a] AED 250,000 is ~USD 68,060
[b] AED 25,000 is ~USD 6,810

Scheme A will only work if either spouse's salary is enough to cover the entire living costs of the household each month.

One of the main advantages of this scheme is that there are no complicated calculations involved. Choose a spouse's salary and do not touch it. Dip from the other spouse's salary for every single need. It is as easy as that.

Table 9. Sample Scheme B dedicating part of both spouses' salaries into the sinking fund for a property down payment (and extras)

Sinking fund for property down payment and extras	Spouse 1's monthly salary	Spouse 2's monthly salary
AED 250,000[a]	AED 25,000[b]	AED 25,000
Contributions	Spouse 1's monthly contribution (in AED)	Spouse 2's monthly contribution (in AED)
Month 1	12,500[c]	12,500
Month 2	12,500	12,500
Month 3	12,500	12,500
Month 4	12,500	12,500
Month 5	12,500	12,500
Month 6	12,500	12,500
Month 7	12,500	12,500
Month 8	12,500	12,500
Month 9	12,500	12,500
Month 10	12,500	12,500
Total	AED 125,000[d]	AED 125,000

[a] AED 250,000 is ~USD 68,060
[b] AED 25,000 is ~USD 6,810
[c] AED 12,500 is ~USD 3,400
[d] AED 125,000 is ~USD 34,030

In Scheme B, both spouses will still be contributing to the monthly living cost, and both must contribute to the sinking fund.

You will still arrive at your target amount within the same duration as Scheme A granted that the salaries between the spouses are somewhat similar and the living costs can be covered by half of each spouse's salary.

What if you are in a one-income household or purchasing a property on your own?

The same strategy applies. Assign a portion of your salary that will go into the sinking fund for the property down payment. If that feels like it will tighten your budget too much, you might need to move around figures and sums across your budget spreadsheet (more about this in Chapter 8) to come up with a monthly amount you can dedicate for your down payment sinking fund.

A property down payment is not something you would usually and regularly have to save up or pay for, hence, during the duration of you accumulating this fund, chances are you might need to give up a little bit of luxury in your life. One or two of your non-negotiables in life might take a back seat for now in lieu of this other bigger non-nego-tiable you are aiming for.

You might also delay adding to your investment accounts by ceasing to contribute entirely until you have come up with your prop-erty down payment, if you want to do it aggressively and come up with the deposit as quickly as you can.

You may also redirect a portion of your usual investment contribu-tion to your property sinking fund if you do not want to lose the opportunity cost of investing your money regularly into the market (or whatever your preferred investment vehicles are). Opportunity cost, in this context means, what you would have given up (income from invested money) in exchange of another thing (down payment for a property).

No matter how you decide to move your money around, just make sure you have enough for your monthly living costs, so you don't feel deprived, and do not touch what is dedicated to your retirement.

You might feel impatient with completing your sinking fund and say, *"What if we have found the property of our dreams and we want to buy it now, but we still do not have our down payment saved up?"*

Or *"Property prices are soaring, and we want to get our foot on the prop-erty market ladder right now. We cannot wait that long to come up with our sinking fund for the deposit!"*

I hear you. Both are completely valid concerns. Some would approach this by reverting to the original plan of paying the least amount of down payment, usually just 5%, as mentioned in Chapter 3. You already know by now what the repercussions of that option are (i.e., the added cost of private mortgage insurance, higher interest payments, or longer borrowing tenure), which don't make it a better option at all. If you can negotiate for better mortgage terms (i.e., no mortgage insurance), or if you can refinance the mortgage down the road with better borrowing terms, then entering the property market even with 5% of down payment just to avoid the impending soaring property prices in the near future might not be such a bad thing.

Remember though, you can never predict the future of the property market. No one can. When a colleague of mine bought a two-bedroom property for investment at ~AED 1,000,000 (~USD 272,260), he was so sure he'd timed his purchase well and from that moment on, the value of his property would increase. However, in a matter of three years, his property devalued to ~AED 800,000 (~USD 217,800) because of the market's drop in demand while properties sprouted up like mushrooms left and right. Nobody was buying, but developers kept building.

It is better to focus on things you can control because no one can predict the upswing or downswing of the property market, just like my colleague couldn't predict that his property would devalue. Perhaps, a few more years down the line, his property will increase in value again. When exactly? Nobody knows because nobody has any control over that. You can control how much you can keep every month from your salary to add to your property down payment sinking fund. You can control your budget to improve your savings rate. You can control how much of a down payment you can save prior to purchasing a property. Focus on what you can control.

Still, for others who are determined to buy now but don't have enough for a deposit, they might take out two loans: a personal loan amounting to the 20% down payment plus extras, and a mortgage to fund the rest of the property payment. This would require simultaneous payment of the personal loan and the mortgage, unless you have a special arrangement with the bank to delay one or the other. And even if they allow one payment to be delayed, it certainly would not be by much. Both loan payments would most certainly overlap. And don't forget that both accrue interest as well, and each deferment of one or both loans will accrue additional interest as the borrowing tenure increases in duration.

Regardless of your decision, make sure your choice is advantageous to you and your household. Remember, one of the reasons you are reading this book is because you want to protect your mental health against financial screw-ups.

If you can come up with a better plan than those suggested above, by all means follow it. Our priority is that none of our financial plans add to our day-to-day challenges and create mental angst. So, take the path of least resistance.

As of writing, we do not have a primary residence yet. But as mentioned earlier, we have started building a sinking fund for our down payment. To be honest, we are still on the fence about owning a property what with all the expenses that come with it like property tax, home ownership insurance and maintenance costs.

Should the time come when we decide to buy a property to use as our primary residence, I plan to create new and separate sinking funds for the annual property tax, home insurance and maintenance, just to be ready.

For a car

Saving up a 20% down payment for a brand-new car is not as hard as saving for a property deposit because the total amount is not as big as that needed to buy a house or a flat.

During big holidays, you might notice that there are a lot of promotional offers for cars. Some of the common offers include packaging free gifts into the buy, adding a year or two of free maintenance services, bundling registration and insurance for the first year, free delivery, and many more.

Another common offer is the famous 0% down payment. Wow! That is really an attractive offer, is it not? Who *doesn't* want to take home a car right at this very instant without having to pay anything upfront? Well, actually, me. And you should not want this scheme too! While this is a very enticing offer, please refrain from taking a bite into it.

0% down payment would mean that you pay a higher interest fee because of the bigger outstanding balance for the tenure of your loan. There is also a possibility of ending up with a balloon payment (recall this concept from Chapter 3). It is best that you pay the recommended down payment, or more if you can before purchasing that car.

As of writing, I don't own a car. There are a number of reasons why I still don't own a car at my age even though I drive and have a licence in my home country. Here are the main three reasons, some of which I mentioned earlier:

- *It is economical and sustainable.* I find taking public transport quite sustainable. I do not have to think about anything (e.g., maintenance, change oil, etc.) except the ticket. The more I can "combo" the ticket (e.g., weekly, monthly), the better!
- *I can dual task.* I love taking public transport especially trains. If it is a long commute, I always have a book to read, so despite others feeling like a public commute is a huge waste of time, for me, it isn't. In an earlier chapter, I mentioned that I carpooled in a Toyota Coaster to work. I remember those commutes to work in Abu Dhabi, it was 45–50 minutes one-way. In a day, I'd spend at least 1.5 hours seated in that Coaster/bus/carpool. Those days, I could easily finish two or three books in a week's commute. I also used to take a nap during my commute in the afternoon. And when I had things to learn, I used my commute time to study. Basically, when I was commuting, I'd be doing two things at once: getting to my destination and reading/sleeping/studying.
- *Previous trauma.* I was in a car accident in the late 2000s. Even though I was just a passenger, the experience made me averse to taking control of any kind of vehicle because of the possibility that I may not do a good job of it. But I'm trying to slowly recondition myself since it has already been quite a long time. And I know that if I take the necessary steps, I can completely get over it.

The reason why I'm saying all the above is because sooner or later, I know that I have to get a car for myself, for one reason or another. And once I own my own car, I would like to add sinking funds for:

- Car insurance
- Car registration
- Driver's licence renewal
- Car maintenance
- Car repair

As you can see, I have separated the car maintenance and car repair funds. The car maintenance is preventive in nature, and it happens on a schedule, regularly and consistently, as you so choose.

However, there are certain circumstances wherein your car would act up and the cost for fixing that is outside of your car maintenance. These circumstances are certainly unexpected. Because we all hate unexpected expenses, it is better to be prepared.

What if my sinking funds are full?

What happens if, after filling up my sinking fund's target amount, I know for sure that I won't be needing the money anytime soon? Should I continue putting money into it?

It is quite possible that an expense you have been saving up for might not end up coming about. For example, you were saving for your health insurance add-ons, but when you switched jobs, your new employer was actually providing a better health insurance plan than your previous employer.

All of a sudden, you have a full sinking fund for health insurance add-ons that you would not need anymore and you do not know what to do with the money. Or perhaps, your upcoming trip was postponed indefinitely due to circumstances that were out of your hands (e.g., a natural calamity, a pandemic). Suddenly, your entire travel fund is full but it will not be spent anytime soon.

What to do with an unused full sinking fund?

Here are some common options that you can do with your sudden "windfall":

1. **Move the amount to another sinking fund that is in need of love.** This will hasten the completion of another sinking fund, or several sinking funds if you decide to distribute the amount to more than one.

2. **Spend half and save the other half.** Enjoy and reward your-self for having this fund completed by spending half of it, and then move the other half to another sinking fund, just like the first option.

3. **Spend all of it**. Why not? It's your money anyway.

4. **Invest everything**. Do this only if it would give you the equivalent feeling of rewarding yourself, just as if you were spending it all on something you need/want.

5. **Spend half and invest the other half**. The benefits of investing are literally far into the future (long-term), so if doing option #4 would make you feel deprived right now or if you need immediate gratification for a job well done, then spend half and invest the other half of your free money.

6. **Leave it untouched**. If the fund stays full, that means part of your monthly income that has been going to this fund during the past few months will be free. Add this surplus to your discretionary fund and feel free to use it in any way you want. Just remember that if this fund stays full for too long, it becomes a lost opportunity cost if you could have invested it instead.

The first five options would require you to start saving up for this fund again should the time come when you need it again. If building up this fund in the past few months didn't feel like an inconvenience to you, then saving up for it again would be chicken feed.

The last option gives you that extra peace of mind knowing that the money is just there.

The choice is completely yours. No matter which option you take, you should feel rewarded because you did the right thing in the months leading up to it. This way, you would not feel as though contributing to your sinking fund is a "chore".

Besides, the entire reason why I'm writing this chapter and the next few chapters is so we can still enjoy our money while at the same time keeping our debt-free status. So, go on. Enjoy your sudden "free" money however you want!

CHAPTER 8
GIVE EVERY BUCK A JOB TO DO

I have been using a budget spreadsheet ever since I started working as an expat. And you would think that would solve all my money problems, right?

Wrong.

The budget spreadsheet only contains numbers, but without the proper mindset embedded into your practice, those numbers will be mere suggestions.

No matter what formula or function you embed in your spreadsheet, no matter how colourful each cell is, it will not matter unless you are really hitting the numbers you have projected.

In this chapter, I'm going to show you how I created a budget spreadsheet that finally works, after multiple iterations! It all came together with two big steps: (1) analysing my previous months' spending, and (2) doing a zero-based budget. But first, let's look at this big F word that personal finance geeks have been tossing around relentlessly. This F bomb is critical to your expense analysis later on.

FRUGALITY IS THE NAME OF THE GAME

If you have been reading a lot about personal finance lately and trying to find answers on how to better manage your money, you would see the word frugality more often than not. It's almost as if personal finance and frugality are inseparable.

Almost all the financial gurus I have encountered through books, podcasts, blogs and other media, recommend being frugal as one of the vital parts of getting out of debt.

Frugality does not mean you will always buy the cheapest thing possible. Frugality has more to do with the economy of your buy than the price you paid for something.

A classic example is buying a piece of furniture that is of good quality and value which will last five years compared to buying a very cheap item for half the price, but you have to replace every year.

If you do a quick search of what frugality means for other people and what they do to practice frugality, some of the most common examples you will come across are:

- bringing a packed lunch to the office instead of eating out;
- less eating out and more cooking and meal planning at home;
- buying timeless pieces of clothing that can be worn regardless of season and current fashion trends;
- buying the flagship unit of a gadget line to have access to all its features now rather than buying it later after not having been satisfied by a lower-tiered product of the same gadget line;
- buying durable – albeit pricey – luggage knowing you will never have to replace it in this lifetime.

Sometimes, frugality is exemplified differently depending on the context, just like when choosing to:

- eat out or order take out for a single person because cooking fresh meals at home is not economical, time and money-wise, if done for just one. In an earlier example, less eating out is viewed as frugal. But in the context of a person cooking for just himself, ordering take out might be more logical as it saves a lot of time shopping for ingredients and cooking. It also is more frugal in this context as the person avoids accumulating unused leftovers for ingredients that can't be purchased in a smaller amount. Workarounds include meal planning and batch cooking if he doesn't mind eating the same dish for the next couple of days.

- buying a used car that can do the job of taking you from point A to B vs. buying a brand new car within your means to have that peace of mind only a brand new car warranty can offer. Buying a used car might be more logical for one person, while avoiding sudden massive repairs for a used car might be more logical for the one who would prefer to buy a brand new car instead.

I would like to think that being frugal is being mindful with my buys. So, how did I find out if I was already living a frugal life or not? I did it by analysing my previous spending habits. The whole process needed only six months of my credit card statements (i.e., three months prior to time of analysis and three months after) and a spreadsheet.

EXPENSE ANALYSIS

As I have mentioned in Chapter 2, all my purchases go through my credit card. This made analysing my spending habits quite easy.

How I analysed my expenses

Step 1. The first thing I did was to extract all my purchases from my credit card statements of the past three months and put them on a blank spreadsheet. Typically, this would have the following columns: (1) the date of purchase or transaction date, (2) the merchandiser or the transaction description, and (3) the amount paid or the transaction amount. Some banks have additional columns like the posting date and foreign currency, but the three mentioned above are all I needed to analyse my spending.

Step 2. I then added a fourth column and named it "Categories". I went through each transaction and provided a category for each. These were the categories I used:

1. *Bills and subscriptions*. This category included all recurring bills like mobile plans, home internet, water, electricity, streaming services (e.g., Netflix), Microsoft Office, Apple Music, Amazon, and more.

2. *Dine-in, take-away, delivery*. This category included all food purchases that I didn't cook. Basically, anything that was purchased from a restaurant, no matter the mode of receiving it, went into this category.

3. *Groceries*. This category was all about purchases of anything I cooked for our daily meals. Medicine and supplements also went here.

4. *Home supplies*. This category included toiletries, cleaning supplies, home fragrance, and all the consumables relating to the upkeep and maintenance of our home. Groceries and home supplies can fall under one category especially if you buy all items from one source. Because we bought all our food from an online grocer and all our home supplies from Amazon, we were able to put them in separate categories which made us track the trend of our food purchases much more easily (our home supplies costs didn't change much).

5. *Shopping*. This category was what I used for all the clothes, shoes, board games, cycling gear, and more.

6. *Transport*. This category included everything related to, well, transport. Monthly bus pass, metro tickets, and more.

7. *Variable*. This category consisted of all purchases that did not fall into any of the above and were not recurring monthly. For example, if I had to process certain documents in a particular

month (e.g., visa or Emirates ID renewal), that went into the variable category.

This categorisation of purchases took a moderate amount of time for me. I had to recall certain purchases because the merchants' names are sometimes not that obvious as to what they are selling. This is why some items took time before I could decide which category they would fall into.

If you are going to do this, make sure you block off enough time to finish it all in one sitting. It could be tedious and time-consuming, but I highly recommend you do *not* skip it. Do *not* even use money apps that will do the categories for you automatically because it defeats the purpose of having to do it manually and waters down the experience.

If you are doing it for you and your partner/household, it would be better if you are sitting with your partner when you do this, so you both get the benefit of this exercise.

What is the benefit of this tedious exercise? A shift in mindset. That is why, no matter how many purchases you must categorise, please do *not* use an app to do it for you.

As you assign categories for the purchases you made in the last three months, you will immediately notice which items are your usual expense "bloaters" – the ones that do not make up your non-negotiables in life (Chapter 4) and do not follow the utilitarian concept which we talked about in Chapter 5.

The next time you see those items in the mall or on your online shopping platform, it will be easier for you to just skip them without debating about whether to get them or not.

Step 3. I added up all the purchases per category to see how much I spent on each per month. It was eye-opening. After finding out what was bloating my expenses, I had to either phase them out of my purchases or remove them cold turkey from that point forward. Looking at those figures, not only did I see where I was spending recklessly, but I instantly knew where I should reduce my expenditures without having to sacrifice anything.

Remember, I promised you at the start of this book that I will not ask you to cut out your favourite daily Starbucks frappe or that you refrain from buying your highly coveted limited-edition sneakers. What good is life if you cannot enjoy your own money? I'm confident to give that advice because, for the purchases that mattered to me, I too didn't cut them out of my budget after analysing my spending habits.

This analysis gave me terrific insights as to why my savings were small even though my income was more than enough. Putting each purchase into a category showed me the expenses that, after carefully deciding whether to keep them or to cut them out of my spending, helped me fix my budgeting. And you know what? After deciding to cut out certain recurring expenses in my life, I didn't even feel like I was missing out on anything. It wasn't an inconvenience at all.

In fact, it even made my quality of life better because I was able to focus on the things and experiences that really mattered, plus the peace of mind it gave by being able to free up a good portion of my income and redirect it towards savings and investments.

Once you see the total of each category for each of the past three months, you can already see the pattern of your spending habits. If not, analyse more than three months' worth of expenses. Some recommend doing the analysis for the past six months or the past two years.

Optional step: And this is what the next three months of credit card statements are for. Continue your life as usual, with the addition of doing Step 2 (categorising your expenses) once each month for the next three months, just to see whether you were really able to cut out the purchases that were bloating your expenses.

Below, Table 10 shows an actual computation of our expenses at the start of 2023 for a household of two adults and one dog. Every now and then, I like to take time analysing our expenses because some-times, we do lose sight of our spending and we end up with a lot of bloaters again, as shown in the first three months in the table below.

From January to March, it's quite obvious that our total monthly expenses were quite erratic. But after doing the analysis, our total expenses were more or less the same for each month from April to June.

We deliberately don't lock ourselves in to spend only a certain amount per category per month. We wing it and just manage to not go above AED 10,000 (~USD 2,700) on average.

Table 10. Six months of categorised expenses

Categories	January	February	March	April	May	June
Bills and subscriptions	1075.87	256.97	646.07	1790.14	683.27	788.15
Dine-in, take-away, delivery	2401.95	4285.62	4530.10	1636.17	2171.21	1159.89
Groceries	2130.89	2201.38	2852.01	632.87	2094.70	3499.32
Home supplies	879.79	742.64	1037.10	610.25	754.47	307.70
Shopping	3591.00	306.00	2973.83	29.99	1186.55	85.00
Transportation	263.40	639.40	175.90	283.45	569.18	631.55
Variable	100.00	420.73	3795.37	2330.15		60.50
Total expense per month	**10442.9**	**8852.74**	**16010.38**	**7313.02**	**7459.38**	**6532.11**

If you have been successful in curbing your unnecessary expenses, you will see a huge leap in your remaining amount, which you can then redirect to your existing sinking funds, which would mean you will fill them up faster. Or you can even create new sinking funds for other projects of yours.

You will only have to do this analysis once. This is just to make sure that your money goes to what truly gives you joy, not financial stress. If you feel like you want to audit your expenses every now and then or at least once a year, you can set a routine date to do so. Perhaps, your birthday so you do not forget it.

In addition to your birthdate being a good reminder, it would also be nice to know your current net worth this year as compared to last year, so you know if the *needle* is moving. If you do not want to do any maths on your birthday, then any day during your birth month would do.

Another time you might need to do this analysis is if you suddenly notice a jump in your expenses that is not attributable to drastic inflation, just like I did in our own sample expense analysis above. If you want me to help you in your expense analysis, you may fill in this online form: https://bit.ly/rian-grace-expense-analysis.

Now that you already know what to get rid of based on your previous expenses, you basically know your actual numbers – your actual living costs minus the bloaters.

At this point, you already know your non-negotiables in life, you already know what you want to build sinking funds for, and you have one credit card that you use for all your purchases. You are now ready to put these numbers altogether in a budgeting scheme known as zero-based budgeting.

ZERO-BASED BUDGETING

Zero-based budgeting (ZBB) is a concept that started in the corporate world in the 1970s.[1] In this half of the chapter, we are going to talk about a different ZBB, one that is appropriate in the context of personal finance.

Simply put, ZBB requires that whatever your income is, when you take out all the expenses, you will be left with *zero*. Does that mean you have to spend all your money? No, silly! It just means you have to give each dirham or dollar a job to do, be it to buy food, pay rent/mortgage, pay for entertainment, or go into your savings account/sinking funds.

What you would need to set up and apply ZBB to your budgeting scheme is your trusty old spreadsheet, the one you have been using over the past few years. If you currently do not have a dedicated budget spreadsheet, go ahead and open a new file right now or add another worksheet in the spreadsheet we used for the expense analysis we did earlier in this chapter. The categorised expenses will be the best basis of how much you will allocate for each aspect of your monthly expenses especially for variable expenses like food, shopping and entertainment. Assigning money for rent/mortgage is the easiest one since we only have one figure for that. Lastly, you have to keep your list of sinking funds handy to complete your ZBB.

Too many spreadsheets!

A friendly reminder: do not make too many spreadsheets related to your finances. If at all possible, use one and keep adding worksheets into it. Personally, I use one spreadsheet file where I have separate worksheets for my sinking funds, my investments, my wish list, and my expenses analysis. Moreover, I have been using the same spreadsheet for over a decade now, archiving certain worksheets that I do not need anymore, or aren't relevant to my current situation anymore. This means I shift old worksheets to another spreadsheet file entitled *Archives.xlsx*. It's where I keep worksheets I don't need to access as often as my current worksheets.

Some readers might call me grandma for using a spreadsheet instead of any of the latest and really helpful budgeting apps available nowadays. But apps come and go, while spreadsheets have been around even since before I was born. It's a timeless tool, hence, my resolve to put everything on a spreadsheet. (As I was writing this, Mint, one of the best budgeting apps for quite some time, has announced they're closing.)

Alternatively, if you don't want to use a spreadsheet, there are many digital applications nowadays that would easily keep these data for you. (I still highly recommend that your expense analysis be done with a spreadsheet or without the help of the automatic categorisation of an app.) Your mobile banking app might even have this feature. You can set your budget allocation in your preferred app and you can set it to notify you when you are running out of money in a certain expense category. It serves as a good reminder if you are spending too fast and depleting a certain allocation well ahead of your next replenishment (salary).

There are also third-party apps that aggregate the inflow and outflow of your money and categorise them automatically. But it requires you allowing them access to the data of your bank account, which for me is a little bit risky. However, if you have vetted the third-party app properly and with enough scrutiny, then feel free to use them at your own discretion. Or you can manually enter your expenses instead.

Regardless of which medium you choose to use for your ZBB, you must have the following categories:

1. **Income**: this is your salary and all your other income from your side hustles or businesses. Basically, anything that is coming in.
2. **Expenses**: this category includes everything that is going out, including intended savings. Remember, this is zero-based budgeting. Whatever portion of your income you assign to savings or investments is deemed "spent".

These two main categories, when added up, should equal zero, or close to zero but not less. Let us practise with a monthly income of AED 15,000 (~USD 4,080).

Table 11. Sample zero-based budgeting of a monthly income of AED 15,000

Income		Expenses	
Salary	AED 15,000	SF: home down payment	2,500
		SF: upcoming winter trip	1,500
		SF: for investment/retirement	3,000
		Rent	3,000
		Utility bills, subscriptions	1,000
		Groceries and eating out	2,000
		Transport	1,000
		Entertainment & discretionary spending	1,000
AED 15,000 (~USD 4,080)		**AED 15,000 (~USD 4,080)**	

SF – sinking funds

For those who have a credit card and who want to maximise earning points for rewards and cashback, here's how it would look like instead:

Table 12. Sample zero-based budgeting of a monthly income of AED 15,000 with all non-rent expenses charged to a credit card

Income		Expenses	
Salary	AED 15,000	SF: home down payment	2,500
		SF: upcoming winter trip	1,500
		SF: for investment/retirement	3,000
		Rent	3,000
		Credit card limit	5,000
AED 15,000 (~USD 4,080)		AED 15,000 (~USD 4,080)	

SF – sinking funds

If you have more sinking funds than shown in the above example, or if you want to further simplify your budget table, you can combine all your sinking funds into one figure and make sure to manage them individually in another worksheet.

Table 13. Sample zero-based budgeting of a monthly income of AED 15,000 with all non-rent expenses charged to a credit card and all sinking funds combined

Income (in AED)		Expenses (in AED)	
Salary	15,000	SF total	7,000
		Rent	3,000
		Credit card limit	5,000
AED 15,000 (~USD 4,080)		AED 15,000 (~USD 4,080)	

SF – sinking funds

If you remember in Chapter 2, one of my recommendations to determine what your credit card limit should be is to make it equal to your monthly income, so that no matter what happens, you always have the ability to pay it all off with one month's salary. My more aggressive recommendation is to have it equal your disposable monthly salary minus your rent and intended savings (all your sinking funds). The latter recommendation is what I applied in the examples above, which means you will have to use your credit card for all your non-rent purchases at any given time.

If your bank delivers SMS for every transaction you make just like all UAE banks, then the latter recommendation also makes monitoring your remaining "money" much easier because every time you use your credit card for any purchase, you receive an SMS from your bank that shows the transaction and also shows your available balance. (If this feature is not a mandatory feature of banks in your country, check if your bank's mobile app allows enabling push notification for each transaction instead.)

With this setup, you do not even need to track your expenses at the microscopic level. You do not even have to be so hard on yourself in situations wherein if you budgeted AED 500 (~USD 140) for dining out this month and you were over by AED 100 (~USD 30), you feel like the whole budget comes crashing down. It doesn't matter if you eat out a little more and spend more than what you intended for dining out in a certain month. What matters more is what you do to balance that out and stay within your credit card limit.

Forget about being so rigid with your allocations. As long as your total expenses for that month are within your credit limit and you have already set aside an amount equivalent to that limit from your salary, then you are fine. Remember to let that amount "stew" in your dedicated sinking fund/e-savers account, to earn a little more interest before being used to pay off your credit card in full before the end of the billing cycle.

This strategy is the reason why I don't have to look at my budget spreadsheet and balance everything down to the last fils or cents. My credit card balance tells me exactly how much more I can spend for the rest of the month, and I get reminded of that balance after every purchase, thanks to our banks sending SMS for every banking transaction that we do.

By simply looking at your available credit card balance and not having to constantly put in your expenses on your money app or budget spreadsheet will definitely reduce the time needed to spend thinking about all this.

You can even add one more step to your recurring money transactions, so you have even fewer things to think about. And what is that step? Automation. Personal finance guru Ramit Sethi, author and host of *I Will Teach You to be Rich*, highly advocates automating your money transactions. You can automate your:

1. **Savings**. In Chapter 7, we talked about opening separate e-savings accounts for each of your sinking funds. Almost all banks nowadays have features that allow you to set a certain amount of money to be transferred from your current account (salaried account) to your appointed e-savings account at a recurring date of your choosing. If you have ten sinking funds to feed each salary time, that might take a while to finish ten transfers between your accounts every month. Automating it would make your life much easier. Just make sure you pick a recurring date that is well after your salary day so your e-savers can pull out the required money.

2. **Payments**. Gone are the days when you had to line up at the bank so you can pay off your monthly bills. You can easily set your credit card to autopay for your electricity, water, cooking gas, internet, mobile, cloud services, and more. This eradicates the worry about late payments and discontinued services. Moreover, with all the subscription-based models of most businesses going on right now, allowing them to bill the subscription amount to your credit card ensures no interruption.

3. **Investments and retirement funds**. If you have brokerage accounts, you may automate them as well so you don't forget setting aside money that works for you and for your future.

Coming from the Philippines where I experienced a handful of faulty charges on my credit card or my phone bill every now and then, I became quite sceptical about the concept of autopayment. I had to make sure first that all the purchases on the statement were legitimate before I could pay off my credit card and phone bills because once you pay them off, it is quite hard to argue for a reversal of faulty and hidden charges.

Thankfully, in the UAE, I have never experienced companies secretly floating hidden charges into my bills, hoping consumers wouldn't notice them. Although, I did experience several fraudulent charges on my credit card, which were reversed promptly by following the recommended ways of reporting such transactions with my bank's representative. I didn't even need to wait to receive my credit card statement to know I had fraudulent charges, thanks to quick and automated banking alerts via SMS.

Automating payments is also quite helpful in not having to memorise each and every due date of your bills and subscriptions. If you do decide to automate, please add a few minutes of your personal finance time each month to double-check if the charges on credit cards and monthly bills are correct. If your statement comes every first day of the month, perhaps you can assign the second day of the month to sit and review your statements, and the third day as your autopay day.

Should you choose not to automate your payments, *most* UAE services (i.e., electricity and water, telecommunications) are billed on the first day of each month and have 15 days after billing as their due date. It's quite easy to remember.

For everything else like your Netflix, cloud services, Microsoft, etc., if you want them all to have the same cycle, unsubscribe to all of them, and then subscribe again on the day of the month you prefer to start their cycle.

Combining those two big steps (three-month expense analysis and zero-based budgeting) led me to create a budget spreadsheet that allowed me to save 50–60% of my income during my last three years of employment in the UAE. Even if I do not add a single buck to that amount, investing and growing those savings, keeping it untouched, will allow me to retire comfortably at 60. Technically speaking, any income that I earn today can be fully spent without having to add anything to my retirement fund, and it would still grow to the amount that I would need to sustain the same lifestyle when I turn 60.

But of course, knowing myself, I cannot imagine not saving just because I already have my safety net. Besides, if I want to add more to it, I can even retire earlier than 60. Ever heard of the FIRE movement? It stands for financial independence, retire early. For more on this, check out the Recommended Reading section. Who knows, it might be something that you'd want to pursue but don't know yet.

CHAPTER 9
AVOID GET-RICH-QUICK SCHEMES

I think all of us have heard this saying more than we ever cared to listen: "If it is too good to be true, then it probably is." I understand the yearning to search for other possible income streams, because at this point, if you already are debt-free and are able to save a lot in addition to your retirement fund, it is logical to find a place where you can park your money and make it work for you. But I do hope we are all careful before giving our hard-earned money and life savings to an investment opportunity just because it promises high returns in a short period of time.

Losing your money to a bad investment because you got carried away by the all-too-good-to-be-true returns is quite devastating. It is all the more overwhelming when the money invested was borrowed to begin with.

Yes, a lot of people borrow money to invest in something they see as irresistible. They cannot let the opportunity train pass by without them getting on board. So, they immediately gather the amount needed, through a personal loan from the bank or by borrowing from family and friends, just so they can buy in to the investment opportunity *now*. Failing to earn from that investment because it tanked hampers you from paying back what you owe the institutions or your family and friends.

Having said that, it doesn't mean it would hurt less if what you invested was your own money (not borrowed). Losing your savings could lead to a series of debts down the road just to recoup your losses, especially if the money you invested was originally earmarked for something else (i.e., for a home deposit; a child's college education).

In either situation, debt is a looming possibility. And we do not want bad debt at this point, because we have worked so hard to get out of it, and we would definitely want to keep our debt-free status. So, how do we make safe investment-related decisions?

There are hundreds of books out there that will give you a definitive guide on where to invest your money. However, in this chapter, I'm not going to tell you where exactly to invest your money, but I'm going to give you a basic guideline as to where *not* to invest your money.

If I'm allowed to give only one piece of investment advice to anyone for the rest of my life, it would be to know how stocks and shares in a business work. I'm not talking about learning the technical terms and jargon about the stock market, Wall Street, and the like. I'm talking about the concept of buying a stake in a certain business. The concept of being a shareholder, and what it means to the business you invest in. You do *not* even have to buy any shares right now.

I know a lot of people who are sceptical of the stock market and about investing in shares. So, I repeat, you do *not* have to buy any shares right now. I just want you to study how it works.

Where does your money go the moment you invest in a business? What is the product or service of that business? How will your invested money earn based on the product or service they are selling? What will the business do with the profits? How will the business keep the investors, like you, happy so you will keep vouching for them (through your invested money)? If you add more money to your investment, where will it go? If the business earns some more, where will the profit go? How does the business grow?

Until and unless you understand how being a shareholder in a business actually works, do *not* invest in any other investment opportunities.

THE ANATOMY OF A BUSINESS AND ITS RELEVANCE TO INVESTORS

We all have eaten out at a restaurant, right? I'm going to assume that at this point, you my reader, have seen a restaurant, at least once in your life, being run as a business. So, let us take the business of a restaurant as an example and dissect what a business needs in order to run. I'm going to oversimplify everything because (a) I'm not a restaurateur, and (b) I want all of us to be on the same page before I tell you what it has got to do with where *not* to invest your money.

To start up a restaurant, the owner would need a massive amount of capital to begin with. Let us take each item needed in a restaurant space by space, as if we are *entering* a restaurant.

First, the venue. Whether the place is built and owned by the restaurant owner, or is being leased, the venue alone would require money. Depending on the location, the cost of build or rent could be higher or lower.

Upon entering the restaurant, you would right away be greeted by the host or hostess, who is salaried of course (another cost). The host/ess would then seat you at your table and hand you the menu. The tables and chairs, tablecloths, crockery, cutlery, glasses and the interior of the restaurant, all cost money. The printing of the menu itself requires money. If it is an electronic menu and is shown on a tablet, that definitely costs money. And if it is a simple online menu accessible through scanning a QR code, it would still cost money to pay the graphic designer for the layout and design of the menu and the professional photographer for the images of the food being offered by the restaurant.

After choosing the dishes you want, the wait staff (or tablet menu) would then inform the kitchen team about your choices so they can start cooking them. And you guessed it right, the kitchen itself costs money! The cooking tools, equipment, supplies, ingredients, condiments, raw materials, cleaning products, lighting, and more. The chefs, cooks, and everyone employed in the restaurant that we haven't mentioned yet, they all cost money for their salaries. Even their uniforms!

We have not even touched on the utility bills for the restaurant to run, marketing and advertising costs, website and social media management, registration, licences, permits, taxes, and more, because these are things we do not normally see as customers as we walk in, sit down and dine at a restaurant. But basically, everything mentioned above is all vital in the running of a restaurant business, from the perspective of a customer. And if we and a lot of other customers liked what we saw, loved what we ate, and enjoyed what we experienced from that restaurant, chances are it will be a profitable business.

So, how does the above example relate to where *not* to invest? I will get there. But first, let us imagine that this restaurant is owned by your friend. And your friend tells you, they are happy with how business is going. In fact, they are so pleased about it that they are planning to offer shares of the restaurant to prospective investors to allow for business expansion.

Your interest is piqued, and you talk some more about the investment opportunity with your friend. You get more excited because you have the money to be a shareholder of a thriving restaurant.

Upon making the investment official, your money becomes part of the pool of money that is used to make the restaurant run or expand. And your invested money can earn in two ways: (1) the *value* of your investment goes up because the overall value of the restaurant goes up and (2) you earn *dividends* from the profit of the restaurant. Both these earnings are commensurate to your investment.

How does the value of the restaurant go up? Remember, we entered and dined at the restaurant earlier, right? We decided to return at a later date for lunch, and we found it was full. There was a wait time of approximately 30 minutes for those without a reservation. Everybody in town is raving about it, and they keep coming back. People from nearby towns are checking it out as well. The restaurant becomes fully booked for the next two weeks, from locals and out-of-towners alike.

The owner is compelled to open a branch in a nearby town. How will this be possible? Through your and all the other shareholders' investment in the restaurant. The money you invested with them could build another wall, buy a few more tables and chairs, purchase a blast freezer, and so on. And since you are not the only shareholder who invested in the restaurant, it is possible to put up a branch from all the investors' pooled money. So, tell me, which was one has a higher value: owning one restaurant or owning two of the same restaurant? No doubt, owning two of the same restaurant is more valuable than one. I told you earlier I would oversimplify the heck out of this example!

As I have mentioned earlier, your stake in your friend's restaurant business is commensurate with the amount you invested. The profit of the restaurant is 100% owned by the shareholders, but it doesn't mean it is 100% provided as dividends. Some of the profit might be redirected for the improvement and upgrades of the restaurant, which further increases the value of the restaurant.

As part owner of the restaurant, your dividend earning is based on the percentage of your ownership of the restaurant. Let me give you a visual example to simplify the concept:

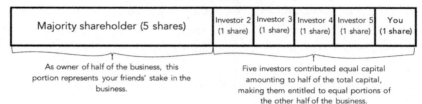

Restaurant shares (10 total shares)

Majority shareholder (5 shares)	Investor 2 (1 share)	Investor 3 (1 share)	Investor 4 (1 share)	Investor 5 (1 share)	You (1 share)

As owner of half of the business, this portion represents your friends' stake in the business.

Five investors contributed equal capital amounting to half of the total capital, making them entitled to equal portions of the other half of the business.

For every 100,000 net earnings of the restaurant

50,000	10,000	10,000	10,000	10,000	Your dividend 10,000

This is assuming 100% of the net earnings is paid to the shareholders as dividend.

e.g., Restaurant earned 486,000 in one year at 30% dividend payout

72,900	14,580	14,580	14,580	14,580	Your dividend 14,580

Not all the time, all earnings are paid out to shareholders. A portion of it (70% in the case above) is reinvested back to the business to further improve or expand it. That becomes part of your total share.

Figure 5. An example as to how dividends are distributed to shareholders based on shares owned (dividend payouts may vary)

But before it could earn, your money must also be used to run the restaurant first. You also partly pay for the operation of the two restaurants because you partly own them. If it branches out again, then your money becomes part of the operation of the third branch and so on and so forth.

If the sales of the restaurants take a hit, your profit takes a hit as well. If the restaurants do well, your profit will do good as well. Unlike a salary though, dividends from investments are not paid that frequently to investors. This would be mentioned in the fine print of your investment papers and could be either quarterly, twice a year, or annually. Very rarely are they distributed to investors on a monthly basis. But I think being paid quarterly, twice a year, or annually makes more sense because if sales tend to vary (i.e., some months have more holidays or public occasions, and that would compel people to dine out more than the other months of the calendar), then taking the average earnings by the quarter, six months, or of the whole year would make the dividends less bumpy.

Regardless, this is not your job as an investor. Your job is to keep your money invested so you keep receiving part of the profits through dividends. And if you do cash out your investment for whatever reason, be sure that the value of your investment has gone up.

Without computing for it, what would be the tell-tale signs that your investment has gone up? Barring debt or any other liabilities, you can easily tell if your investment in the restaurant business has gone up if it branches out some more. The bigger the expansion, the higher the value, especially if the investment required to put up branch number three, four, five, and so on have already been recouped. And this will take some time, so as an investor, patience really is a virtue. You cannot jump on board and expect that next year, your money has already doubled, especially if most of the investors' money is still being used to purchase more equipment or expand the operations.

Now you have a basic idea of what is needed to run a business, let us try and dissect one more example before we relate this to all other investments. We have all been to a grocery store, right? Let us make this simple by looking at one aspect of the store that could help increase its value and profit: the freezers.

All grocery stores have freezers which hold the food items they sell. The more freezers a store has, the higher the expenses will be (i.e., the cost of buying the freezer unit and the cost of running it with electricity, not to mention its maintenance costs). But the more freezers the store has, the more they can hold perishable goods to sell as well. The more items the store can sell, the more profits.

If the store adds one more freezer, yes, it will be an added expense again, but it will also allow more room for food to be kept by the store, and later sold. Through the sales, the cost of the additional freezer can be recouped in due time. It does not get any simpler than that.

Have you ever noticed a grocery that has closed down few years after it has opened? What were the signs that it wasn't thriving? Perhaps, there was less food on display and a lot of items that were out of stock for an indefinite period of time. Who would want to shop at such a grocery store? It doesn't appeal to customers, right? So, it is losing more customers by the day, until it finally closes down.

In contrast, a well-stocked grocery store, one with lots of food items for sale, one that keeps on expanding, will always get visits from regular customers because they know that what they need is always available in that store.

THE ANTIDOTE TO GET-RICH-QUICK SCHEMES

Now, we get to apply the concept of being a shareholder, based on the examples above, in trying to avoid sketchy investments. As a shareholder, you should *know* where your invested money goes.

Earlier, we explored where money is needed and how that money is used to earn more money. We learned that setting up a business has its inherent value from all the tools, intellect and manpower bought by the capital, and that as long as it keeps operating, it will earn profits which could be reinvested into the business to further increase its value or be distributed to investors in the form of dividends. Just keeping all these components of business and shares in mind will help you answer if a certain investment opportunity that is being offered to you is legitimate or not.

To know if an investment opportunity is sketchy or not, ask yourself the following questions:

1. **Are they promising high returns for a short period of time?**
   Doubling our money overnight is just so damn irresistible, right? Who wouldn't want that return on investment (ROI)? Some people get roped into such investment scams because they'd rather be oblivious to the risk, hoping to wake up freaking rich! Remember, to dream is free, so never allow your dreams to cost so much money that you'd be willing to lose your life savings on the off chance that your wishful thinking of doubling your money overnight is true. If you're still not convinced that such high-return-short-period gimmicks are a bull, try looking up how long before Warren

Buffett, Jeff Bezos and Bill Gates got to see returns on their investments.

2. **Where does the value of the business lie?** What is the equivalent to their *dining tables, chairs and chefs,* which we described in our restaurant example? What is the business's *freezer* equivalent based on our grocery store example? Of course, don't ask these specific questions to anyone offering you an investment opportunity, especially if the investment opportunity you are eyeing up has nothing to do with restaurants and grocery stores. You just have to open up your mind and reflect what your money represents in the hands of the person offering the investment. For example, if the investment proposal is so abstract that you cannot comprehend what your money would buy for the company or business you're investing in, perhaps, it is better to back off from the opportunity. Investing your money should be so simple that you should be able to explain it to a ten-year-old. You don't need to understand complex concepts just to understand where your money goes. If the investment proponent cannot help you understand what the business is for, remember that you are not stupid, they probably are just sketchy!

Let's take a look at some common methods of how we could get swindled into investing our money in different investment opportunities, and how to avoid them of course!

PONZI SCHEMES

In reality, no one who invites you to invest in their "business" will tell you that they're running a Ponzi scheme. They have to gain your trust in order for this scheme to work (true for most scams). And you wouldn't know what is wrong with this investment until the end of the long game of con. (Con is short for confidence, which is the whole basis of the scheme. They can only swindle you after they have gained your confidence and trust.)

The objective of "Ponzi schemers" is to convince you to invest your money in them, hook you into keeping your money invested by giving you gargantuan returns in a short period of time, make you addicted to the awesome returns so you invest some more money in them, until they disappear.

But where do they get the returns they have given you in the first place? From people like you who believed in them as well. They give "earlier" investors the sign-up fees of "later" investors and they keep this charade going on until the word is out about how successful the "earlier" investors are. This news encourages more people to sign up and invest with them, not knowing that the success of the earlier investors is just a setup to gain the trust of more investors.

How to avoid Ponzi schemes

Before investing, ask the following:

1. **Where will the fund manager invest your money?** They should be able to name specific businesses where your money will go. If this is a legitimate investment, it is not that hard to name the investment ventures. Ideally, these ventures should be included in the fine print of your signed investment papers. If they cannot divulge this bit of information and they just keep on reassuring you that your money is in good hands, you better think twice about entrusting your money to them. Remember the restaurant business as an example, and all the components needed to build that restaurant up and keep it running. A legitimate investment should more or less have the same components (e.g., just replace the kitchen with computers if it is a tech business, you get my point). Common sense is a very important requirement here. So, your money should be used for something that requires capital for physical infrastructure (or online infrastructure if it's a completely online business) and the hiring of talent and manpower. If your money just multiplies on its own without any of the usual business components, you better ask yourself how this happens. And even though it is quite easy to get carried away with the gains *right now*, you can be sure they will dry up soon, perhaps even when you are

way too invested, and you end up losing a lot more. Money invested in nothing *cannot* multiply on its own.

2. **When will you start seeing gains?** Knowing where your money is invested will also give you a realistic timeline on how much your money will grow in months, years, or decades (if you are in it for the long haul). Going back to the restaurant example, each and every night the restaurant closes, the owner does not necessarily provide you with your share of the profit right away. Not even at the end of each month. Sometimes, it could be within a quarter, twice a year, or once a year. Investing in individual stocks and index funds does not make anyone an automatic millionaire overnight, unless it is the lottery (which is technically not an investment vehicle and should not be), which brings us to the third thing you need to ask.

3. **What size gains are we expecting?** If the fund manager promises stellar returns of investment in a couple of months, for example, double or triple your investment amount, then it is time to rethink this venture, especially if the gains are out of nothing (if they cannot divulge the investment vehicles they will be pursuing) based on their answer to the first question above.

PUMP AND DUMP SCHEMES

Just like Ponzi schemes, no one will approach you and outright ask you to invest in their pump and dump (P&D) schemes, which means you have to do your due diligence to avoid getting roped into one of these schemes. What are pump and dump schemes?

P&D is a form of price manipulation that involves artificially inflating (pump) an asset's price before selling (dump) the cheaply purchased asset at a higher price. Once the assets are "dumped", the price falls and investors lose money.[1]

This scheme used to be common among stocks, and the practice was perpetuated by insider trading wherein the very few who know (insiders) are at an advantage of earning money as they know the perfect time to sell (dump) compared to the "outsiders" who bought and made the stock price soar only to wake up to their investment losing its value when the insiders sell their shares.

With the crackdown on insider trading, this scheme has happened less and less in the stock market over the years. I guess it helps that insider trading is actually considered a felony and not only requires paying massive fines (up to AED 1,000,000 or ~USD 272,260), but also jail time of up to three years. Although, you can bet that it still happens from time to time.

Nowadays, P&D schemes have become quite popular in the cryptocurrency world.[2] Before I proceed, I want to be extra clear that I'm not against cryptocurrency, blockchain, deregulation, or anything that is remotely related to cryptocurrency. But I'm completely against the gimmicks being made surrounding this investment vehicle. That's why I'm including it on the list of investment schemes to be aware of so you can save yourself the headache of being scammed and losing a lot of your hard-earned money.

P&D schemes work well on investments whose prices can easily be manipulated. Such is true for companies, products, or stocks whose values are blindly overestimated by investors. P&D perpetrators could easily sell a certain stock as "the next big thing" and everyone would want a piece of it, buy shares of it immediately for the fear of missing out, and cause the value of the said stock to soar.

What most people do not know is that behind this "rockstar" stock are criminals who are waiting for you to put your money in, and once you and others have driven the value up to their desired amount (pump), they then begin selling their shares (dump).

The pumping could happen in days, weeks, months, even years. But the dumping could happen in a matter of seconds or minutes, and if you're not aware of it (of course you wouldn't, because the information on *when to sell* is exclusive to the perpetrators of this scheme), by the time you start selling yours, the value will be lower than when you bought your shares. And that is how to lose your money in ten seconds.

But how is it even possible to devalue a company or stock that quickly? The answer is because it may not have any intrinsic value to begin with.

How to avoid pump and dump schemes

Before investing, research deep and wide about the asset you are about to invest in, and ask the following:

1. What is the asset's intrinsic value? An asset's intrinsic value is linked to its future cash inflow. If the asset you are investing in is truly legitimate and is not a vehicle for pump and dump schemes, you can analyse this through publicly available documents about the asset, be it a company, a product, or a stock. And if investors know that a certain asset's future cash flow is excellent and reliable, why would they pull their money out, right? Who in their right mind would suddenly pull out their investments from an asset that would genuinely grow in value and bring in dividends, unless it is a pump and dump scheme!

2. Is it possible to wipe out the intrinsic value of this asset overnight? This relates more to volatility: the degree of upward and downward swinging of an asset's price. If you are rooting for an investment opportunity wherein you think you can make a lot of money on its upward swing, just remember that you are equally vulnerable to its downward swing. And more often than not, an asset that has no intrinsic value could be subject to more volatility.

Let's take McDonald's as an example. Even without looking at its books, we know that it has an excellent cash flow in the near and far future. If you buy McDonald's shares right now at USD 250 a share, rest assured that when you wake up tomorrow, it will not be USD -3. You cannot devalue an asset like McDonald's just like that, unlike the shares being sold in pump and dump schemes.

As long as all McDonald's outlets are up and running, it will continue to bring in that intrinsic value we were talking about earlier, and it is quite hard to wipe that value out in under 24 hours. As long as all McDonald's branches are operational, the cash inflow from each and every burger and soda they sell feeds the company's intrinsic value consistently thus safeguarding its stock price from dipping down so low.

If you have been reading more about stocks and the whole market as investment vehicles, you'd know by now that dips in the stock market are normal occurrences. It could be due to any factor like market correction, economic depression, recession, shift in supply and demand, or a combination of any of these. But those dips in the market are nothing compared to massive drops in pump and dump schemes. So be very wary of where you'll be putting your money.

Examine every angle of the asset and should due diligence make you decide it is a *plausible* investment, only put in an amount you are willing to lose. If it turns out that it is indeed a pump and dump scheme, you will only lose the amount of money you are willing to part from.

Trust me, even renowned personal finance and investment gurus dip their toes in novel investment vehicles or emerging markets. But they do it with caution and they only invest what they can afford to lose because they know that volatility is a bitch. If you see their portfolio (some of them are quite transparent about their allocations), you can see that investments towards cryptocurrency for example is a measly 5% of their entire portfolio. You will also notice that their portfolio is well diversified enough to ride out any bad investment they may have. But because they are already seasoned investors, they already have a keen set of eyes against investment scams such as pump and dump schemes.

PYRAMID SCHEMES

I have a confession to make. I sincerely hate businesses operating under the guise of a pyramid scheme. There! I said it. Let my family and friends who have been in one (or two or three or more) hate me. I've been asked numerous times to join someone's newfound "business" which was clearly a pyramid scheme. How do I know? Because they want to recruit me as a member, that's how!

Just like Ponzi schemes, pyramid schemes rely on the *confidence* of the investors that their investment would make huge returns (more like unrealistic, but they don't know that yet). Their difference lies in the fact that pyramid schemes require investors to recruit more "investors".

Before proceeding, I believe it's important that we clarify something first with regard to the similarity (or difference) between pyramid schemes and multi-level marketing (MLM).[3] In multi-level marketing, yes there is also membership. Yes, there is also recruitment of new members. But the focal point is on the products to be sold.

The products are not necessarily sold to members only, but to the general public who might need a solution for their problem. Think of Tupperware, a household products company that sells food preparation, storage and serving solutions. In its earlier business format, it utilised a multi-level marketing strategy. Or picture Avon Products, Inc. Founded in 1886, Avon is one of the oldest companies in the cosmetics industry. Its business model is also based on a multi-level marketing strategy.

Based on Tupperware and Avon as examples, there are real products to be sold with real value (especially back in the day when they held most of the market without much competition). The profit comes from sales to the general public, not based on how many people you recruit to be your downline.

With pyramid schemes your earnings as a member come from a cut of the membership fee of the person you recruited under your name. If your recruit in turn recruits more people under their name, you also get a small cut from that. And so on and so forth.

If pyramid schemes and MLMs are different from each other, would I invest in an MLM business then? It's a hard no for me as well. With the massive improvement in capitalism and distribution over the years, I don't think I'd ever need to be a member (or buy from a member) of a certain company to simply gain access to certain products that I need. Just consider this: even Tupperware, a company that's been popularised by its MLM strategy, has since adopted direct distributorship to provide in-store purchasing of their products.

When I was still living in the Philippines, I got to attend to a few of these pyramid scheme "talks". But do not judge me because I was only there under the guise of an old friend's invite:

"Hi Rian. It's been long since we last saw each other. Do you want to grab dinner sometime next week?"

After the said dinner:

"Would you like to go to this business talk that my colleague is having? It's just down the block, and it will not take more than 30 minutes."

Okay, who am I to say no to a short business talk, right? I'm anyway open-minded.* Wink! (Spoiler alert: it was neither a legit business talk nor did it last for less than 30 minutes!)

So, there I was, in a crowded hall with hundreds of other unsuspecting prospective pyramid recruits, waiting for the "talk" to start. To entice people to sign up with the business, they present a person who is like the "messiah" of that particular pyramid scheme – I mean, business. Excuse me, Freudian slip.

They usually pick someone with a rags-to-riches success story so the masses can relate to them. It is important to emphasise that the success was solely because the messiah joined the business they are selling.

Usually, they would come to the event while everyone is just gathering up outside the hall. This is perfectly timed because they want to show possible recruits their luxury car (usually a Jaguar) as they get dropped off by their driver. The messiah would wave and smile to the gathered crowd to get more attention while his car is still there.

Of course, you as a new person there, won't know who the hell this person is, but your friend who brought you there will surely tell you who that person is. Later during the talk, expect the messiah to mention that if it weren't for his profits from joining the business, he will never be able to afford that Jaguar (or whatever luxury car they thought of renting that night).

---

* This is in reference to the usual opening line of pyramid scheme recruiters: "Are you open-minded?" It has been an inside joke among those who have been scammed or almost scammed.

In one event that I attended (the one where I had dinner with a friend and all of a sudden, I'm attending a "business talk"), the messiah's Jaguar still had all the plastic cover on its seats and head rests. I'm not sure how luxury cars are sold, I've never bought one. But if it comes without plastic covers, then they went to a lot of effort to cover the inside of his Jaguar with plastic sheets! Maybe they were trying to prevent getting the seats soiled as they still needed to return it to the dealer later that night.

I swear, there's just too much effort on their part to "sell" that the pyramid messiah is someone we all have to emulate so we can also get our own Jaguar. One time, the same messiah with a plastic-covered Jaguar seats was selling it so hard, he even picked up a phonebook, showed his surname in one of the pages just to show us his address *Tondo*, a very sketchy neighbourhood in the metropolis where squatters and looters abound, to make a point that he indeed grew up poor. I could see the desperation on his face to sell his rags-to-riches story, insisting that we too could achieve all the things he had achieved if we became a member of their "business".

What else did I learn during these talks? If you get recruited, you get to be a part of the downline of your sponsor, the person who invited you to join the business. You being a member generates an income for them because they take a portion of the membership fee you paid, and give it to your sponsor, and the rest are similarly divided up to your sponsor's sponsor, and your sponsor's sponsor's sponsor. You know where I'm going with this, right?

When you start recruiting people, you now have your own downline. You start earning as soon as you recruit someone to be part of your downline. The more you recruit, the more membership fees paid, the more income you get. But wait, there's more! (Spoken like a true commercial!) In some pyramid schemes, they employ bonus incentives if you pair up your downline, if you get a combo recruit that looks like the encircled portion in Figure 6, or whatever scheme they want to add, so recruiting gets more enticing. The gimmicks are endless!

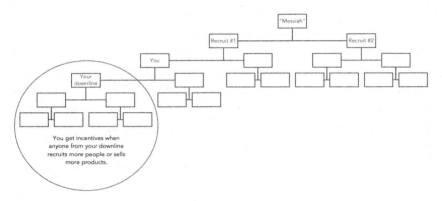

| Figure 6. A typical pyramid recruitment scheme

Not only are there endless gimmicks, perpetrators have also found a way to make themselves look like a legitimate multi-level marketing business (recall that they are not the same). They bring in products and include them in the membership "package" to disguise themselves as MLM. The presence of products makes the members look like legit "distributors" so when they peddle around recruiting new members, they won't look like a pyramid scheme because they do have products to push, just like Avon or Tupperware.

With all my personal stories above about pyramid schemes, you might already be itching to say, *"Hey, Rian. For someone who hates pyramid schemes, you sure have been to a lot of their business talks!"*

Yeah, well, I was textbook people pleaser when I was younger. So, as long as I could delay saying no to anyone, I would. I always dreaded saying no to a friend or a relative who was trying to recruit me. I hate pyramid schemes and their intention, but I don't hate my friends or relatives who have joined them. At the end of the day, those who join such schemes are all about earning a little something on the side, right? I'm just happy I don't have pushy friends and relatives and they understand when I say no. Although now I'm older (and hopefully wiser), I know how to say no right from the bat, so as not to waste my time and their time too.

You might be wondering, *"Why don't you just teach your friends and relatives about the dangers of joining such schemes, to prevent the possibility of losing their hard-earned money or life savings?"*

First, they have never asked my opinion about whether it is a good idea to join one of the above schemes or not. They just join. I'm a firm believer in not giving unsolicited advice,* in any aspect of life. You see, when someone invests in something they truly believe in, no amount of advice or convincing will make them want to back out. They have done their due diligence and they are ready for all the promised glory of the business. Contradicting their decision will only make you look like a villain plotting against their plan to get rich!

Second, if they ask me about legitimate investment vehicles, they don't follow through. A former colleague of mine asked me where I invest my money so she can do the same. We were both about to take our six-week-long annual leave and she was planning to invest some of her money when she visited her hometown during our vacation.

I told her I buy shares of long-standing dull businesses † through their cooperatives or through the stock market. I explained to her how the whole thing works. She asked, *"How much do you earn from all of these?"* I told her, *"I don't really look at the earnings right now because I don't need them right now. I can still work and I can use my current salary to provide for myself at that moment, so there's really no need to count earnings of my investment and spend them."*

I explained further that I picked these investment vehicles to hold my money on a long-term period so that when I retire, I can access them at the value they've grown into, including the dividends. She wasn't that happy to hear that because she wanted to invest in some-

---

* Why not give unsolicited advice? Because people think you know better than them. If you give them any advice without waiting for them to ask for it, you assume they know nothing about what you wanted to tell them. It's short of saying, *"You don't know this, so you better listen to me!"* It never sounds nice. By the way, this book does not count as unsolicited advice because you picked this up yourself. I didn't force my way into your thoughts and say, *"Hey, go buy my book and follow each and every piece of advice written in there to a T!"* 😉

† I learned the phrase from Thomas J. Stanley and William D. Danko's phenomenal book, *The Millionaire Next Door*. In the book, they listed common businesses where millionaires in the US invest their time and money. They were dubbed as "dull-normal" because, while nothing is exciting about them, they do perform quite consistently well. A few examples of these businesses are janitorial services-contractors, long-term care facilities, and manufacturing. To find out the rest of the list, don't forget to add *The Millionaire Next Door* to your reading list and read up!

that would give her big returns right away, not when she retired. She wanted to spend the earnings right away, on top of her usual income.

I did tell her also that in one hospital cooperative I bought shares in, me and my family are entitled to use the hospital services at an investor's rate, which are heavily discounted as compared to the general public for the obvious reason that I'm a shareholder in that hospital – technically a part-owner to simplify terms. That somehow answered her question as to what *now* benefits I get from my non-stock market investments. (I got the feeling that somehow, she was averse to investing in securities and she didn't want to spend a single minute learning more about them.)

After returning from our annual leaves and back to our ordinary lives at work, I was curious as to which investment vehicles she had chosen so I asked her, with the assurance that she didn't have to share this information with me if she wasn't comfortable divulging it. She happily and proudly answered my question by saying, *"I bought gold through Emgoldex. I even bought each and every member of my family shares in it. We already have the gold certificate!"*

I think my jaw was way down to the floor as she was saying this, because she reacted defensively to my non-verbal expression. I don't know what I looked like at that specific moment, but I have been told here and there throughout my life that I have facial expressions that could hurt like a dagger. And that's probably why she immediately went into defensive mode, citing all benefits of her investments, and how she and her family were ahead of everyone else when it came to actual wealth.

I didn't mean to offend her with my reaction, I was just sincerely in awe of her decision, despite everything we'd talked about before we went our separate ways prior to our vacation.

In short, advice is not sought when about to invest in something sketchy, and advice is not followed when people are taught of legitimate investment vehicles. When someone wants to invest in something they believe will make them extremely wealthy, let them. And if that investment goes south, they can charge their losses to experience.

Speaking of losses, I think it's time to get real. One study stated that a whopping 88% of participants lose their money in pyramid schemes.[4] Another study based on a survey stated that only 25% of MLM participants earned a profit while the rest lost their money or broke even.[5] Make of that what you will.

A word of caution, friends. When you know someone in your circle of people who is knowledgeable in matters like these, talk to them. Inquire about things you don't understand, because, though people shouldn't be giving unsolicited advice, people love to answer questions and share what they know. That's everyone's default, or at least the sincere ones. If you ask them any questions about what they are geeking about, they will happily answer them for you. But please, do not ask a million questions only to do the complete opposite of what they've talked to you about. That's not inquiring; that's just pestering!

How to avoid pyramid schemes

Compared to Ponzi and P&D schemes mentioned earlier, I think pyramid schemes are glaringly obvious. It's not so complicated to spot one.

1. **Watch out for the red flag terms.** During the first meeting itself, the word "recruit" and "downline" get thrown in frequently during orientation. There could be products packaged into the membership, but this could be a ruse to make it look like a legitimate MLM business.

2. **If there is a product involved, check if it is of real value and are truly beneficial to consumers.** If yes, is being a member of this "business" the only way to access these products? As an example, an obvious pyramid scheme was founded in the Philippines some time in 2015 and was targeting Filipino expatriates because of their earning power. They even had a high-profile MLM person endorse the whole "business". Of course, granted that he accumulated a large portion of his wealth through MLMs, a lot of people wanted to follow suit. What was the product of the company? They were selling services such as money remittances, mobile phone reloading and bills payment. If you notice, all these services are existing businesses and are already accessible to the general public without the need to pay for an exclusive membership. But the

selling point of their scheme was that as a member, you'll get exclusive discounts and rebates on all these services, and you get to be a distributor of these services. This means you earn more on top of your "bonuses" from recruiting more people into the "business". If you truly are convinced of the benefits of signing up to this business, do the maths. If your membership fee is just breaking even with the income from all your recruits and rebates after years of being a member (if the company still exists by then), then you already know the answer whether to go ahead and give them your money or not.

3. **Check if the income is commensurate with the effort you're willing to put in or is required of you.** I know some people who quit their jobs to focus full time on recruiting members to be part of their downline (and selling the products and services to appear like a legitimate MLM business). But wasn't this supposed to be a side hustle? Or a passive income from recruitments made by your downline? Isn't recruiting two members under you enough to generate for you multiple incomes from the people they will be recruiting under them too? Somehow, the maths doesn't add up there. But if you remember our "messiah" earlier, he or she gets to benefit from all the new recruits because he is at the top of the pyramid, how come you don't get enough from the people-below-the-people you've recruited? Are you getting enough hints already? Perhaps, it's time to pull the plug because you know it isn't working anymore. It suddenly becomes more work that you didn't sign up for, something you might not be willing to do.

TIME-SHARING "ASSETS"

One day during a vacation, while my cousin and I were enjoying the white sand and the view of the pristine waters of Boracay, one of the many beautiful islands in the Philippines, a member of staff from a high-end waterfront hotel near our spot approached us and invited us to an exclusive dinner buffet at the fancy hotel's terrace. She said it was free and we just had to bring the stubs she just handed to us. She was distributing them to other tourists as well. And when other tourists heard of it, they came to her and asked for their free dinner stubs too. Who says no to an upscale restaurant at a five-star hotel's free dinner buffet, right?

Because we hadn't scheduled anything for that night, we decided we might as well pop by and see what the fuss was all about. In my head, if it turned out to be a recruitment scheme, at least we'd get an awesome dinner for our troubles.

As it turned out, the free dinner was indeed a ruse to "corral" unsuspecting prospective recruits into a time-sharing business talk. This was back when time-sharing "businesses" were starting to boom. So, I genuinely had no idea the free dinner buffet invitation was for the sake of luring possible recruits in. (To be fair, it was an awesome dinner buffet!)

After the exclusive dinner, everyone was encouraged to stay for another hour or so to hear their business pitch. What they were offering was very lucrative especially for travel bunnies like me: a chance to share ownership of vacation properties across the Philippines and in select parts of the world.

The sales agent (let's call her Shelly) assigned to our table was really convincing. (There were two other ladies at our table that night, so the sales agent-client ratio was 1:4.) Shelly was this sweet and patient lady who talked eloquently about the offer. Shelly was not aggressive at all (unlike the pyramid scheme guy I mentioned earlier) which made her all the more convincing. My cousin almost signed up! Shelly was that good.

No matter what Shelly said though, my mind was already made up the moment she sat across our table. Nay, the moment our dinner buffet ended, and they started announcing the real reason why they had invited us there. First of all, the deception threw me off. So, it was a hard pass for me.

That was my very first time attending a time-sharing talk. (*"Goodness, Rian! How many times did you get lured into attending such events?!"* I hear you ask.) Don't worry, it was just that one time in the Philippines. And another one in the UAE, with a completely different strategy to lure possible recruits in (more on this later).

But again, no matter how many times I attend these talks, my ability to say no to things I don't believe in never diminishes. I can't part with such a huge amount of money (membership and maintenance fees to these time-sharing deals cost an arm and a leg) to a company I haven't vetted myself. I need time and deep research to know more about the company before I entrust a single dollar to them.

It doesn't help that they make us decide whether to join in or not right at that very moment. If I'm backed to a corner by a huge business conglomerate waiting for me to decide whether I'm in or out with only seconds to spare, my answer will always be a no. And yours should too.

See, they create this illusion of *scarcity* by telling us that their irresistible offer – of "owning" our own vacation properties in different parts of the Philippines and the world – will only last the same night. Shelly said that the moment we stepped out of the hotel that night, the offer ceased. And should we decide to go for it, we had to make a down payment of USD 1,000 right there and then (besides the massive annual "maintenance" fees).

By the way, if you want to learn more about *influence,* Dr Robert Cialdini's book entitled *Psychology of Persuasion* details the six cardinal principles of influence, one of which is, you guessed it right, *scarcity*! Knowing how you are influenced by others could be a game-changer when it comes to your decision-making process for any investment-related matters.

So, did my cousin buy this time-share offer? Nope. The other two ladies at our table bought the offer though. They hurriedly created a plan as to which (and how many) among their credit cards they were going to use to make the down payment.

Twelve years later, in the UAE, I experienced attending a similar "talk" where they were selling time-share vacation properties and travel packages. This time, the invitation was hidden under the guise of invitees winning a raffle entry. The raffle was legit. There was a ticket involved. There were prizes too. But winning the raffle included an ulterior motive which of course, nobody knew about until claiming time.

How did we get the raffle ticket? My partner and I were having lunch at a restaurant chain in Dubai one time. A restaurant staff (or so we thought) approached us and told us that with the amount we had ordered for lunch, we were entitled to a raffle ticket which could win us a four-day, three-night staycation and a dinner dhow cruise. It only required one of our names and a mobile number. I quickly wrote my name and mobile number on the ticket, separated my claim stub, and gave back the ticket to the staff.

Two days after, I was informed I had won the raffle. They gave me an address where I could claim my prizes. It was a ballroom in a known hotel in Dubai. They required that upon claiming the prizes, I should bring my partner with me. Okay. Not at all weird. I just assumed they probably wanted a photo opportunity with all the winners and their plus ones. (Photo opportunities with raffle winners are quite a common practice in the UAE. But then it is usually for big ticket winners only like someone winning AED 1,000,000 [~USD 272,260] or a Tesla or any luxury car.) So, that was my first mistake. I dismissed a few weird requirements like the prizes having to be claimed the same day (they didn't give any other option) and the spouse's presence.

My second mistake was that I didn't do any background checks against the company providing the prizes. It certainly wasn't the restaurant. The name of the company was related to travel, and I thought, *"Okay, the restaurant must've outsourced the prizes to a travel company because the prizes are related to travel. There's nothing weird about that."*

I was on a summer break at that time while my partner was working. In hindsight, I must have really wanted to simply get out of the house. And when they contacted me to claim my prize, it gave me a reason to get out of the house. So out I went without even reading about the company.

Lo and behold, the person who gave us the raffle tickets wasn't even a staff of the restaurant where we dined (shame on that restaurant for perpetuating that "raffle" on their property just so another business could collect contact details of prospective recruits. At the end of the day, businesses would really do anything to get more business without any regard to their clients' privacy and safety against scams).

We entered a ballroom of the hotel address given to me. There were a lot of people inside, seated around tables in a 1:2 ratio (one agent per two "raffle winners") and it looked like their discussions about the prizes had begun way ahead of ours.

We were seated with a fellow-Filipina lady. Let's call her Cindy. She explained we would be receiving our prizes momentarily but asked us to allow her 30 minutes of our time to listen to her pitch.

Thus began another time-share sales pitch, this time with flight and tours included. But even before it began, my partner and I both knew our answer was a hard no. Were we brutal enough to let Cindy go on and on about their products knowing that we wouldn't say yes to her? Well, that's the price they pay for luring people into their sales pitch. They'd already gone to great lengths to bring us there, so why wouldn't we let her do her work?

Attending that sales pitch, I noticed massive differences in their setup compared to the one I attended in Boracay 12 years earlier. First, the whole ballroom was filled with the blasting sound of pop songs, so much so that Cindy was almost shouting her pitch to us. I think they deliberately made the music so loud so we couldn't hear what other people at other tables were talking about.

Second, we might have been the only two real prospective recruits that night. The rest of the tables looked odd in that the agent and the "raffle winners" were just casually chatting, not like our table where we had an over-eager Cindy who was trying hard to convince me and my partner to sign up.

At some point, the other "raffle winners" were acting as if they were choosing something on a printed paper being presented by their agent. After a few seconds, the music would get cut and the agent would stand up to announce to the entire hall: *"Let's welcome our new family member, Mr and Mrs Patel!"* to indicate that Mr and Mrs Patel had bought their travel and time-share packages. They did this a few times across different tables while we were there. Perhaps, this was another tactic to show that other people were signing up for membership. They even did it in strategic intervals to build pressure on us.

One similar thing they had with the Boracay time-share I attended before was the sense of scarcity that demanded us to make an urgent decision right there and then.

How did they inject the sense of scarcity into their gimmick?

They told us they exclusively conduct business-to-business (B2B) sales only and that we were lucky enough to be offered their services individually for a limited time period. Another gimmick to create a sense of exclusivity. But of course, we didn't buy into it.

So, did we get our prizes of staycation and cruise even after saying no multiple times to them? Yes! Cindy even had the audacity to call it *their gifts to us*, probably because she was so bitter that we didn't buy into their business. You see, earlier they kept referring to them as "prizes". If it had been a legitimate raffle draw, they'd never have called them gifts. But we already knew their tactic and they couldn't guilt trip us into accepting their "gifts" without being a member of their business.

Did we use the gift? Nope. Not at all. In hindsight though, we could have gifted it to somebody else who needed a break. Maybe in our next attendance, I'll just collect "gifts" and give them all away to my friends and relatives.

How not to get sucked into a time-share sales pitch

1. **When you mysteriously win a raffle you don't remember joining, run in the other direction!** My experience at the restaurant chain above was believable because I did join a raffle. There was indeed a ticket. There were actual prizes. But months after this, I received a call from another travel company telling me I'd won prizes similar to the one I'd won above. Here's how the conversation went:

Me: I'm sorry, how did you get my name and contact details? I don't remember joining any raffle recently.

Caller: You recently shopped at [grocery store chain here] and your raffle ticket got picked.

Me: No, I'm certain I didn't enter any raffle draw. I'm 100% certain because I don't buy groceries at that shop. (It's true that I have never been to the shop he was telling me about. Our groceries are 100% delivered to our home every Monday and I only buy online from this shop called Kibson's.)

Caller: You must have just forgotten.

Me: (Wow. He had the nerve to re-write my memory just so he could lure me into their scam! He is not letting go of me that easily. He wants to trick me, so I decided to waste his time.) Okay. Send me the address of where I should pick up my prizes.

Caller: Okay, I'll send it via WhatsApp including the time. The prizes can only be claimed today. (Here we go again with the sense of urgency and scarcity!) Please make sure to show up at your designated time because that slot is reserved only for you.

Me: Oh sure, sure.

After hanging up and receiving the location via WhatsApp, I blocked him. He must have tried calling me again around the time I was supposed to be there, but because I blocked his number earlier, another number under the same company name, tried calling me instead. They wasted that spot on me. But I was afraid for all the others who weren't able to escape their clutches.

I surmised it was the same company as before, which was why they still had my name and number on file. They must have probably registered under a different company name after losing their reputation from hundreds of complaints filed against them by clients who wanted their money back after not being able to book their vacation properties, flights and tour packages with them.

2. **Reddit is your best friend when it comes to digging information about unknown companies or possible scams.** I'm afraid that in another two or five or ten years, the people behind this kind of businesses will find another way that's different to a luxurious dinner buffet or winning a raffle draw to lure people into their sales pitch. I have no way of predicting their future strategies, but you can always look it up before going to such events. Don't be like me who got lured into another time-share sales pitch just because I wanted to get out of the house. Boredom never did anyone any good! Why Reddit? Because of the anonymity of the *Redditors*. Digging about the travel agency who offered us the time-share packages in Dubai, we uncovered posts of people who experienced dealing and buying packages from the same company, through the same *modus operandi* (i.e., they won a raffle draw). When they were about to use the services for one of their vacations, the travel company did not provide the said services. Instead, they told their members to pay for the vacation first and they will reimburse them later. When the unhappy time-share members decided to cancel their membership and asked for a refund, they were met with resistance, followed by an approval but with a hefty cancellation fee, and a non-disclosure agreement that states once the cancellation and refund were completed, ex-members cannot review them on any social media platform, Google or any service rating platforms. That's why these ex-members decided to warn people against such scams through Reddit, where they can keep their anonymity.

3. **Time is not of the essence in situations like this. Just ignore their deadline.** My cousin was able to say no to that time-share deal in that fancy hotel with the fancy dinner buffet because her husband was able to convince her that the offer was bull. After calling her spouse and discussing the offer with him highlighting the fact that the offer was available that night only, her spouse, like

me was thrown off by the offer. He said to my cousin, *"If it's a genuine offer that is genuinely beneficial to any client, they will actually make it available 24/7 and indefinitely."* Would I have bought into this offer even if they had given me enough time to decide? My answer would still be a big fat no. I couldn't see my money growing in it. There was just no evident growth in value and inflow of dividends.

CRYPTOCURRENCY TRADING PLATFORM/APP SCAMS

Before our cryptocurrency-loving readers throw my book away, let me clarify right away that this part is not about or against the concept of cryptocurrency. It's about the predatory platforms that "sell" cryptocurrency.

Too many platforms and apps popped up at the rise of cryptocurrency. But not all of them were legitimate. When a lot of people put their money in, the proponent suddenly disappeared.

Others lost their login details or forgot their passwords and couldn't access their accounts anymore.

What's shocking is that some platforms don't even have a way to withdraw their investments! It's as if, while blinded by the prospects of high returns, you keep putting your money in, and when it's time to cash them out, you find out there's no way to get out!

When some of my friends got drawn into cryptocurrency investments on various platforms, I asked them to try to withdraw a portion of their investment just to see if there was really a way out. If there was, then it made the platform a little bit more trustworthy than others. One friend didn't want to withdraw a portion of his cryptocurrency investment because he didn't want to "disturb" his portfolio. The other one didn't withdraw as well, but instead asked the customer service of the app what the steps were if investors wanted to cash out. He was satisfied with that already.

Still, knowing how to withdraw an investment by theory is not equivalent to actually trying it. I don't know what happened to my friends' cryptocurrency investments on their respective platforms, but at some point, they stopped being giddy and speaking about it. Perhaps, their investment tanked. Perhaps, they were able to get out before the cryptocurrency value went down and have amassed a great fortune. I don't know, and I'm afraid to ask.

How to be on guard against scamming cryptocurrency trading platforms

1. Look up the platform and go with trusted ones only. Do your due diligence to search for information about the trading platform, how long they've been around, how happy their clients are, and if they are truly vetted by the trades commission of your country.

2. Never hand your money directly to someone who says they would do the trading for you. In short, don't be gullible. If you're going to do this because you really trust the person, always ask for receipts of transactions, or draw up agreements and have them signed by both parties. Always!

3. Check if the platform has account recovery methods in place. Better yet, test it by pretending to have forgotten your password or login details. True set-and-forget trading platforms would have ways to recover login details especially if the user hasn't checked in with their investments for quite some time. That's why it's called set and forget.

4. Start investing with a small amount and then try their withdrawal mechanism. Remember, you can't just keep on dumping your money into a platform without knowing how to take it out (or checking if there is even a way to take it out). As an example, my stocks trading platform in the Philippines allows me to sell shares on the spot and move the amount directly to my bank account. It should be this easy for you to sell a part of your investments and receive the income from the sale as well.

5. Be on guard against promises of high returns in a short period of time. This has been the whole foundation of this chapter and I've been repeating this over and over again. No investment platform can predict the future, so promises about future returns can never be guaranteed.

Sometimes, some investment scams do not entail losing a big chunk of money. Some scammers ask for a very nominal fee that most people would readily get on board with, without batting an eyelash because the money they have to put in is so small that it makes the risk inconsequential. But it is not only the amount you lose in fake investments that we are concerned about here. It is the possibility of going into a spiral of debt because you want to recoup what you lost, or you want to pay off the person/institution whom you borrowed the money from. And you're back to square one again.

I'm debt-free and I keep myself debt-free because I avoid impulsively buying into "exclusive" investment opportunities. They would always stir a sense of urgency inside you, along the lines of, *"It would be such a shame if you pass up this opportunity to sign up with us, because after today, we will not be able to offer you this investment opportunity anymore."* They would guilt trip you into losing a lot of money because you didn't sign up with them. It sounds something like, *"It would be such a shame you won't get to enjoy the profits and benefits of this business in the future."*

Just remember, if it's too good to be true, it probably is!

CHAPTER 10
CONCLUSION

During this "in between" time of mine, a lot of people asked me why I was doing it.

Why did you stop working?
Why are you taking a sabbatical?
What are you doing now?

These were just some of the most common questions I encountered during my year-long break away from employment. At first, I tried to give them the lengthy and elaborate explanations to as simple as, "*I just want to rest.*"

No matter what I said, a lot of them still couldn't fathom why. A colleague even asked me why I was giving up my employment, with a look of worry as if I may never find one like it again.

The concept of taking time away from work seemed alien to almost everyone around me. And as my sabbatical went on, I realised, I'm not taking it because of the reasons I mentioned earlier. I was taking time away from work because I'm *free*. It all boils down to having that option and taking it as you please.

If I need time to pursue my personal projects, I can take the option to just focus on them and not have to worry about my bills. If I need time to study again, I can take the option to completely dedicate my time to that.

Of course, there are those who are also free but would rather keep their current job because they have a healthy working environment and they don't have to run away from it to protect their mental health. That, too, is a fantastic option! But remember, an option – any option for that matter – can only be taken if it is *available*. Let's revisit our unhealthy and anxiety-inducing money and debt-related narratives from Chapter 1 and see how we can reshape them to have a more positive option in life based on the lessons from the preceding chapters about changing money mindsets and managing our debts.

"I feel anxious whenever I open my banking app and I see that
my balance is low on my checking and saving accounts.
Add to that the high outstanding balances on my credit
cards and my anxiety goes through the roof."

You can only take the option to be anxiety-free when it comes to money matters if you manage your finances well. Analyse your expenses, make a budget, pay off your debts, then when you finally achieve that peace of mind from being debt-free, save and invest.

"Ugh. It's Monday again! I don't want to go to work! If only I
didn't have bills and debts to pay, I could just quit right
now!"

You can only take the option to not hate Mondays if you are in a job that you love and pays the bills at the same time, not in a job that just pays the bills. Always aim to be on top of your finances and avoid accumulating debt so you are not forced to stay in a job that would make you hate Mondays.

"I hate my job. I have a terrible boss and my colleagues are not making the working environment any better. It also looks like I'm not getting promoted any time soon, if at all. But I have to suck it up and stay in this dead-end job because I have an EMI for my personal loan/mortgage/car loan, and I still have loads of credit card debt to pay off. Plus, I don't see any other employer that would pay the same amount of salary I'm getting right now."

We can never choose what kind of boss we have in every job we get, neither can we pick who our colleagues are going to be. But we can always choose to walk away from such situations. In order to walk away from a job that is not serving your mental health, you have to have your finances in order. Do not let your finances be the shackle that would prevent you from walking away from your dead-end job. You have to have a big enough emergency fund – enough to cover all your monthly payables so you can take the option to walk away should the need to transition to a better working environment arise.

"I was about to fly off to another country for a leisure trip, but I got stopped at the airport because I didn't pass immigration control. Apparently, I'm on a travel ban list because of my mounds of unpaid debt."

You can only rid your life of this massive inconvenience (and possibly, a very public humiliation) if you choose to manage your money well. Massive debt has ripple effects outside yourself and your family. When you have massive unpaid debts, you don't only have to manage your own money, you also need to pacify the big financial institutions and the government.

> *"I want to transition to another career that I'm more*
> *passionate about. But I have to study for it, and I don't*
> *have enough savings to quit my current job and put myself*
> *through school. I wish I had enough emergency funding for*
> *situations like this."*

Or, in a similar vein:

> *"I want to open up a business about something that I'm*
> *passionate about. But I don't have enough savings to quit*
> *my current job and have enough capital for the business. I*
> *wish I had enough emergency funding for situations like*
> *this."*

If you've reached this far, that means you've already read the answers to your woes in the earlier sections of this book. Analyse your spending, abruptly stop all spends that don't spark any happiness in you, and redirect all that extra money towards eliminating your debt and then saving. When you do all these things, you're not only choosing to be debt-free, you're also choosing yourself!

> *"I don't have any savings or funds for my retirement. I keep on*
> *using up all my salary to pay for my credit cards and*
> *personal loan. Nothing gets left for savings and the future.*
> *But I'm cool with that, because as long as I keep on work-*
> *ing, I will have money coming in and I'll be able to afford*
> *my lifestyle. However, if I lose my job, it's going to be a*
> *struggle until I find a new one."*

If you are cool with this setup, then nothing others say will ever change your mind. But should money anxiety start to set in, you're welcome to reread this book, especially Sections II and III.

"I can't help myself in buying the latest things on the market,
from shoes to bags to mobile phones. I've got to have all the
latest gadgets and fashion trends as soon as they are
released. I sometimes worry about my maxed-out credit
cards, but I can't give up my lifestyle because my friends
would think I'm poor if I don't have all this bling."

Take the option to respect your anxiety. Find your non-negotiables in life. Continue to keep yourself happy with your non-negotiables in life. Stop trying to impress people with what you have. Remember, they can't appreciate your material possessions. They're too busy collecting theirs.

"I have enough disposable income to afford a little luxury here
and there. I'm not in any kind of debt. However, whenever I
do buy luxury items and pay for luxurious experiences, I
feel uncomfortable because at the back of my mind, I keep
thinking I could have added it to my retirement fund/prop-
erty deposit/business capital."

Appreciate the privilege to be able to pay for and enjoy luxury in life. Then appreciate that you have the metacognition (the awareness and understanding of one's own thought processes) to actually decide to use this money for something else, something more substantial, or something income-generating. Use that metacognition to your advantage and act on it.

"I don't need to do anything with my debt at all. I've accepted
that having a lot of debt is normal. Everyone has it."

A lot of people who have been in debt for most of their life have accepted the normality of it. Some of them even make fun of frugal/debt-free people because of the penny pinching and belt-tightening feats they momentarily do while trying to get out of debt. Their favourite line towards frugal people is *"Live a little!"* overlooking the fact that frugal people are doing that so they can live more – get out of debt, stop spending money on useless-for-them things, and start spending money unapologetically on the things they cannot live without. What's worse is that when a debt-free person takes unconventional decisions in life, for example, taking time off work to travel for three months, they would fire criticisms left and right, making sarcastic comments like, *"If only everyone had the capacity to take time off work and not earn money for a couple of months..."* or, *"Not everyone can do this, so get off your high horse..."* If you are one of these people, first, you really don't have to shame people who can choose to take time off work because they've got their money situation under control. Second, try being one of them instead and you will see why a lot of people want to get off the debt train! (Disregard the second tip if you truly are fine living with debt and it doesn't bother you.)

"It's normal for me to have debt because I have a family. If I were single, I could manage my income better. You, on the other hand, can easily save money because you don't have kids."

It is not about being single or being child-free. My sister and her husband have three kids and a person under their employ, and they've never been in debt their entire relationship. They use credit cards and they pay them off in full every month. They bought properties back home and they were able to pay them off without taking personal loans in the UAE. And being single has nothing to do with better income management. How sure are you that if you were single right now, you'd have a better money mindset?

THE ESSENCE OF IT ALL

It dawned on me that our financial problems are not only because of a lack of money – a lot of high-income people are neck-deep in debt – but also because of a deep-seated wrong mindset about money coupled with poor management skills. We tried addressing the wrong money and consumption mindset in Chapter 4 when I encouraged you to reflect on knowing yourself and what you truly desire by identifying your non-negotiables in life, devoid of influence from people around you. But we have not given enough emphasis on how management skills come into the frame.

If you think about it, each and every piece of advice in this book requires you to manage something. Budgeting requires that you manage your income and that it balances with your expenses. Sinking funds require you to manage different "pockets" of money earmarked for future use. Avoiding get-rich-quick schemes require you to manage all the information you have, gather all the information you still need, and decide accordingly. Applying for any type of loan requires you to present all the evidence that will prove you're eligible for that loan, and gathering evidence and presenting it in an organised manner requires you to be adept at managing your important documents. It is quite evident that personal finance is a management game. If you ignore honing your management skills, then chances are it may impact your personal life too, including how you handle your finances.

A lot of people would say they're in crippling debt or they suck at managing their finances because it was never taught in school. It was never a part of any of our curricula growing up. Some also blame their parents for not giving them the slightest idea on how to manage money. While all of these are true, there comes a point in our lives when the blaming of others for our financial issues isn't the solution. You can blame all you want, but it will never take your debts away.

In the capitalist world we live in right now, those who benefit mostly from it – the corporations, the investors, the government – will want us to keep on buying and consuming. The more recklessly we do it, the more they profit. If these bodies include personal finance in our curricula growing up, then how can they earn above and beyond their expectations?

What's stopping you from controlling your debt right now? Are you afraid the economy will collapse if we all become frugal because no one is spending their money? Are you thinking that investors and business owners will go bankrupt from all of us being frugal? That's far from reality.

Even if we all become mindful of our spending and be enlightened with how to manage debt, the economy will still thrive. We still need to eat, we still need to power our houses, we still need connectivity, we still need to clothe ourselves, plus, we still have our non-negotiables to spend on. We will still consume, so businesses will still be alive. It's the *overconsumption* that puts us in debt and lines the capitalist overlords' pockets even more, at the expense of our mental health and peace of mind. And with that stress comes more unnecessary spending which leads to more debt for us and more profit for the super wealthy. It even perpetuates the old maxim that the rich are getting richer and the poor are getting poorer.

If you consume just enough and avoid lifestyle creep, then you're halfway to keeping yourself debt-free. Let's normalise healthy personal finance practices so we can always have the option to be free!

WHAT'S NEXT?

Three words: stay the course. When old habits of overspending are brewing within you, stay the course. When you get impatient while waiting to achieve your financial goals, stay the course. When the allure of keeping up with the latest whatnots gets too tempting, stay the course.

Amidst the sea of *hyper-consumerism* all over the world, it's quite easy to lapse into senseless spending and, eventually, another downward spiral of stupid debts. But always remember, being debt-free in this day and age is an extraordinary flex. It's something everyone can be, but not everyone can do. So, stay the course!

No matter where you are right now in your own personal finance journey, please know that you got this! Best wishes to all of us!

RECOMMENDED READING

1. Benson, Paul. *Financial autonomy: The money book that gives you choice*. Highett, VIC: Major Street Publishing, 2020.
2. Bogle, John C. *The Little Book of Common Sense Investing: The Only Way to Guarantee Your Fair Share of Stock Market Returns (Little Books. Big Profits)*. Wiley, 2017.
3. Cagan, Michele, and Elisabeth Lariviere. *The Infographic Guide to Personal Finance: A visual reference for everything you need to know*. New York: Adams Media, an imprint of Simon & Schuster, Inc., 2017.
4. Campbell, Canna. *The $1000 project: An easy guide to mindful saving and financial wellbeing*. Melbourne, VIC: Penguin Random House Australia Pty Ltd, 2018.
5. Cialdini, Robert B. *Influence, New and Expanded: The Psychology of Persuasion*. New York: Harper Business, 2021.
6. Collins, JL L. *The Simple Path to Wealth: Your road map to financial independence and a rich, free life*. United States: JL Collins LLC, 2016.
7. Devine, Victoria. *Investing with She's on the Money: Build your future wealth*. S.l.: Penguin, 2023.

8. Dunlap, Tori. *Financial Feminist: Overcome the Patriarchy's Bullsh*t to Master Your Money and Build a Life You Love.* US: Dey Street Books, 2023.

9. Freeman Publications. *Stock Investing for Beginners: Fantastic Moats and Where to Find Them - How to Beat the Market Year After Year & Achieve Financial Freedom By Investing Like The Best In The World (Stock Investing 101).* Freeman Publications, 2021.

10. Housel, Morgan. *The Psychology of Money: Timeless lessons on wealth, greed, and happiness.* United Kingdom: Pan Macmillan UK, 2023.

11. Kiyosaki, Robert T. *Rich Dad Poor Dad: What the Rich Teach Their Kids About Money That the Poor and Middle Class Do Not!* Scottsdale, AZ: Plata Publishing, 2022.

12. McCallum, Kate, and Julia Newbould. *The Joy of Money: The Australian Woman's Guide to Financial Independence.* Sydney, NSW: Bauer Media Books, 2020.

13. Mill, Alfred, and Michelle Cagan. *Personal Finance 101: From Saving and Investing to Taxes and Loans, an Essential Primer on Personal Finance.* New York: Adams Media, 2020.

14. Osborne, AJ. *The Investors Guide to Growing Wealth in Self Storage: The Step-By-Step Playbook for Turning a Real Estate Asset Into a Thriving Self Storage Business.* JamesBrennae Publishing, 2020.

15. Pape, Scott. *The barefoot investor: The Only Money Guide you'll ever need.* Milton, QLD: John Wiley & Sons Australia, Ltd, 2022.

16. Rieckens, Scott. *Playing with FIRE (Financial Independence Retire Early): How Far Would You Go for Financial Freedom?* Novato, CA: New World Library, 2019.

17. Robin, Vicki, and Joe Dominguez. *Your Money or Your Life: 9 Steps to Transforming Your Relationship with Money and Achieving Financial Independence.* New York: Penguin Books, 2018.

18. Rodgers, Rachel. *We Should All Be Millionaires: A Woman's*

Guide to Earning More, Building Wealth, and Gaining Economic Power. United States: HarperCollins Leadership, 2021.

19. Sethi, Ramit. *I Will Teach You to be Rich: No guilt. No excuses. No B.S. Just a 6-Week Program that Works*. 2nd ed. Workman Publishing Company, 2019.

20. Stanley, Thomas J., and William D. Danko. *The Millionaire Next Door: The Surprising Secrets of America's Wealthy*. Taylor Trade Publishing, 2010.

21. Thornhill, Peter. *Motivated Money 6th Edition: Sound Financial Advice for the Post-GFC World*. 6th ed. Gordon, NSW: Motivated Money, 2020.

NOTES

4. IDENTIFYING MY NON-NEGOTIABLES IN LIFE

1. Mackesy, Charlie. *The Boy, the Mole, the Fox and the Horse*. London: Ebury Press, 2022.

5. USING THE UTILITARIAN PREMISE

1. Source: The (Mostly) Simple Life
2. Source: The Lady

7. CREATE SINKING FUNDS FOR RECURRING EXPENSES AND LIFE PROJECTS

1. Johnson, Dixie Porter, and Richard Widdows. "Emergency Fund Levels of Households." *The Proceedings of the American Council on Consumer Interests 31th Annual Conference*, 1985, 235–41.
2. Chang, Y. Regina, Sherman D. Hanna, and Jessie X. Fan. "Emergency fund levels: Is household behavior rational?." *Financial Counseling and Planning* (1997).; DeVaney, Sharon A. "Emergency fund adequacy among US households in 1977 and 1989." *Consumer Interests Annual* 41 (1995): 222-223.; Hanna, Sherman, and Hui Wang. "The adequacy of emergency funds to cover household expenditures." *Consumer Interests Annual* 41, no. 1 (1995): 224-225.
3. Rodriquez-Flores, Alicia, and Sharon A. DeVaney. "The effect of employment status on households'emergency funds." *Journal of Personal Finance* 5, no. 4 (2007): 67.
4. Anong, Sophia T., and Sharon A. DeVaney. "Determinants of adequate emergency funds including the effects of seeking professional advice and industry affiliation." *Family and Consumer Sciences Research Journal* 38, no. 4 (2010): 405-419.
5. Lee, Sunwoo Tessa, and Sherman D. Hanna. "What, Me Worry? Financial Knowledge Overconfidence and the Perception of Emergency Fund Needs." *Journal of Financial Counseling and Planning* 33, no. 1 (April 22, 2022): 140–55. https://doi.org/10.1891/jfcp-2021-0045.
6. Johnson, Dixie Porter, and Richard Widdows. "Emergency Fund Levels of Households." *The Proceedings of the American Council on Consumer Interests 31th Annual Conference*, 1985, 235–41.

8. GIVE EVERY BUCK A JOB TO DO

1. Source: McKinsey & Company

9. AVOID GET-RICH-QUICK SCHEMES

1. Li, Tao, Donghwa Shin, and Baolian Wang. "Cryptocurrency Pump-and-Dump Schemes." *SSRN Electronic Journal*, February 10, 2021. https://doi.org/10.2139/ssrn.3267041.
2. Badawi, Emad, and Guy-Vincent Jourdan. "Cryptocurrencies Emerging Threats and Defensive Mechanisms: A Systematic Literature Review." *IEEE Access* 8 (October 29, 2020): 200021–37. https://doi.org/10.1109/access.2020.3034816.
3. Vander Nat, Peter J., and William W. Keep. "Marketing Fraud: An Approach for Differentiating Multilevel Marketing from Pyramid Schemes." *Journal of Public Policy & Marketing* 21, no. 1 (April 2002): 139–51. https://doi.org/10.1509/jppm.21.1.139.17603.
4. Kell, Tyler, Haaroon Yousaf, Sarah Allen, Sarah Meiklejohn, and Ari Juels. "Forsage: Anatomy of a Smart-Contract Pyramid Scheme." *Financial Cryptography and Data Security*, December 1, 2023, 241–58. https://doi.org/10.1007/978-3-031-47751-5_14.
5. DeLiema, Marguerite, Doug Shadel, Amy Nofziger, and Karla Pak. Rep. *AARP Study of Multilevel Marketing: Profiling Participants and Their Experiences in Direct Sales*. Washington DC: AARP Research and Strategic Analysis, 2018.

ABOUT THE AUTHOR

Rian Grace is a personal finance geek. She loves playing board games, reading books, and following *Union Cycliste Internationale* events.

ALSO BY RIAN GRACE

Printed in Great Britain
by Amazon

44066013R00119